"I've seldom read a book more timely and welcome than *The Long Goodbye* by Margaret Miles. That is not to suggest it is easy on either the heart or the mind, or spiritually edifying in any obvious way. No. Miles, although immersed in the history of Christian thought and art, tells of one specific experience of dementia—centering on her late husband, a theologian. She writes with a kind of particularity and unflinching but loving realism that is truly rare. This is not a story told in such terms or details by biblical writers or ancient philosophers or even authors from a century ago. Relying partly on her diary, and interspersing her narrative with poetic quotations, Miles reminds us that dementia is an increasingly modern condition, as populations live longer. Keenly and caringly, she makes clear that dementia is something that changes not just the 'patient' but the lives of all involved. Miles rejects venerable oppositions between original sin and basic innocence, arguing that it is misleading even to ask whether a human being is naturally good or naturally bad. That cannot possibly do justice to the complex reality revealed in a mind beyond mending but not entirely beyond meeting. Along the way, one must learn which self, which other, can still be loved. And finally, Miles helps us ponder what to bring to such love and memory, and into what encompassing reality one is to commend life—any life, all of life—in the end."

—Frank Burch Brown, Senior Editor in Religion and the Arts, *Oxford Research Encyclopedia of Religion*; F. D. Kershner Professor of Religion and the Arts, Emeritus, Christian Theological Seminary

The Long Goodbye

The Long Goodbye

Dementia Diaries

Margaret R. Miles

CASCADE *Books* • Eugene, Oregon

THE LONG GOODBYE
Dementia Diaries

Cascade Books
An Imprint of Wipf and Stock Publishers
199 W. 8th Ave., Suite 3
Eugene, OR 97401

www.wipfandstock.com

PAPERBACK ISBN: 978-1-4982-8238-3
HARDCOVER ISBN: 978-1-4982-8240-6
EBOOK ISBN: 978-1-4982-8239-0

Cataloguing-in-Publication data:

Names: Miles, Margaret R. (Margaret Ruth), 1937–

Title: The long goodbye : dementia diaries / Margaret R. Miles.

Description: Eugene, OR : Cascade Books, 2017. Includes bibliographical references.

Identifiers: ISBN 978-1-4982-8238-3 (paperback) | ISBN 978-1-4982-8240-6 (hardcover) | ISBN 978-1-4982-8239-0 (ebook)

Subjects: LCSH: Thomas, Owen C., 1922–2015. | Dementia—Patients—Family relationships. | Dementia—Patients—Care.

Classification: RC523 .M55 2017 (print) | RC523 .M55 (ebook)

Manufactured in the U.S.A. JANUARY 27, 2017

For the caring caregivers in the Recollections unit at
The Berkshire, Berkeley, California,
2014–2015

CONTENTS

ACKNOWLEDGMENTS

I AM GRATEFUL FOR the skill of doctors, nurses, and hospice caregivers who, informed by knowledge and experience, took time to think hard and carefully about what might help Owen. This book is dedicated to the caregivers who compassionately provided for the daily needs, accidents, and emergencies of residents of The Berkshire Recollections unit, 2014–15.

I am thankful for the "fellow pilgrims" at the Berkshire, thankful for the "beauty of the way and the goodness of the wayfarers."[1] Family members of the residents became friends: Michael, Deirdre, Brian and Julianne. And I appreciate the friendship of residents: Joe, Margaret, Dorothy, Mary Alice, Caroline, Phillip, and Frank.

My gratitude to Professor Martha Stortz for her thoughtful and helpful suggestions for knitting the manuscript, to Charlie Collier, my gentle editor at Cascade Books, and to the Wipf and Stock team. Because of them I must differ with Anne Lamott's aphorism "Publishing isn't all it's cracked up to be—but writing *is*."[2] With the generous skill of the W&S team, publishing, like writing, *is* what it's cracked up to be.

1. Beckett, "Waiting for Godot," Act One.
2. Lamott, *Bird by Bird*, xxvi.

PRELUDE

> Life is too short to devote much of it to activities that are not at the heart of what it is to be human.
>
> —Martha Nussbaum

Owen and I met in 1978 in Cambridge, Massachusetts, shortly after I moved across the country from Berkeley, California, to accept a position at Harvard University Divinity School. I was forty-two. I had married twice, divorced twice, raised children, and completed my doctorate in History the year before. Owen was a tenured Professor of twentieth-century Theology and Philosophy at the Episcopal Divinity School. He was also an Episcopal priest; he had a summer parish, but his career was primarily in the academy. I was hired at entrance level, an Assistant Professor, subject to review and either promotion or termination after seven years. I was scared. I had not published anything, and I feared that colleagues and students would readily recognize that I did not know everything I needed to know to teach "The History of Christian Thought" (100 CE to approximately 1800), the course for which I had been hired.

Owen had known my colleagues for many years; his children had grown up with their children. He thought of them as interesting people, simply "folks." His attitude brought relief to my insecurity as a new teacher. It helped me enormously in my first years at Harvard as I lectured on historical authors and events, some of which I had hastily researched the evening before class. One day Owen appeared at my door with an armload of books he thought I'd find useful for the topic of the next lecture. For the first time in my life I had met a man who was not jealous of my work! I began to love him, and he, recently divorced, began to love me. As my mother used to say, "One thing led to another," and we were married three years later.

Together we had five children between the ages of twenty-three and twenty-five; my daughter and son were on the West Coast, Owen's twins were on the East Coast, his younger son in Europe and then Brazil.

> The world is a smiling place.
>
> —AUGUSTINE

Between 1981, when we were married, and approximately 2005 when I began to worry about his odd behavior, we had a rich marriage. We were critical friends, reading and commenting on each other's writing, which eventuated in positively reviewed publications. We traveled—sabbaticals in Rome and Bolinas, California; two month-long fellowships at Bellagio, Italy; and several glorious vacations in Greece with colleagues. In 1985 I became the first tenured woman at the Harvard Divinity School. In 1996 after Owen's retirement, we moved to Berkeley where I became Dean of the Graduate Theological Union. I wanted to see both sides of the academy, teaching and administration. In Owen's retirement he produced important work in Science and Theology. My retirement in 2002 freed me to concentrate on writing.

Shortly after my retirement, however, Owen began to show signs of dementia, which is where this story begins.

Chapter 1

INTRODUCTION

> Perhaps everything terrible is, in its deepest being, something helpless that wants our help.
>
> —Rilke

Owen's neurologist said, "Now that we can do something to prevent or cure strokes, heart attacks, and even cancer, we are *all* going to live out into the dementia years. The public should know more about it." If loving a dementia patient were simply my personal difficulty I would cope as best I could, but would not write a book about it. But dementia is not only a personal problem; it is also a social problem. At present writing the National Institutes of Health (NIH) reports five million cases of dementia in the United States; the World Health Organization (WHO) estimates 35.6 million people with the disease worldwide. Although we tend to equate dementia with Alzheimer's disease, there are many varieties of dementia. Alzheimer's patients comprise only 50 to 70 percent of dementia cases.

Dementia is not a new disease, but it was named and its characteristics mapped rather recently. Formerly family members who had dementia were thought of as senile and kept privately in the home. It was only when the critical mass of "baby boomers" approached the dementia years that it became a newly *public* disease.

Friends frequently advised me to join a group for dementia caregivers so that I understand that I am "not alone." In the words of a Bob Dylan song, "I know you've suffered much, but in this you are not so unique."[1] I can see the benefit of realizing that I am not unique; it curbs my tendency to narcissistic whining. But why should the suffering of others comfort me? I *wish* others did not suffer. Loving someone with dementia has both a personal and particular dimension and a common, even universal dimension. It is possible that dementia is one aspect of social experience that is not culturally specific. Reflecting on the social dimension of "my" problem has hidden benefits. Thinking of dementia as a social problem places a certain distance between my subjective experience and the disease. Stepping back just far enough from the overwhelming immediacy of dementia—the (sometimes literal) shit and the piss of it—to consider its social dimensions helps to lighten the personal sadness of involvement with a dementia patient, dearly loved but frequently immensely frustrating.

Families of dementia patients have stories—shockingly uncharacteristic ways their loved one has acted, horrific anecdotes, and humorous incidents—if only one can laugh. I learned the importance of laughter from the daughter of an Alzheimer's patient who told me, laughing, that her mother had urinated in the wastebasket. I said, "Oh that is terrible; that isn't funny." She replied firmly, "Yes, you have to laugh at everything you possibly can!" Her wisdom later proved true in my own experience with a dementia patient.

Dementia is not usually treated as a source of valuable learning, insight, and understanding. Indeed, I confess that at certain moments I would have gladly foregone the learning in exchange for eliminating the experience of losing my companion. As my husband's dementia increased, I came to realize that my love for him had become very similar to the love I experienced long ago for my little children, a love characterized by feelings of protectiveness, gentle touching, and eagerness to find and supply experiences that would delight them. Perhaps the primary difference between

1. Bob Dylan, "Dear Landlord."

my little children and my husband was that children learn from their small accidents to avoid large accidents. At a certain stage, dementia patients do not learn from their accidents. Owen did not learn from his many bruises, scrapes, cuts, and falls to move more slowly, to use the walker, and to wear the padded helmet designed to protect his head when he fell.

Caregivers learn that at a certain stage twenty-four/seven vigilance is required, vigilance that is impossible for a single caregiver. The realization that I was unable to care for Owen at home occurred when he adopted a twenty-four hour clock. He slept for a couple of hours; was awake for several hours; then slept again for perhaps four hours; then was awake again and potentially dangerous to himself and others—around the clock. At that point it became necessary to surrender my earlier assumption that I would always be able to care for him at home. I needed sleep and could not adapt to sleeping when Owen slept and waking when he did—around the clock.

I called a family conference. Three of our fifty-something "children" from earlier marriages were able to attend. I anticipated with dread a meeting in which I expected that we would need to rehearse for Owen his recent odd, inappropriate, and dangerous behavior in order to convince him that he should enter a residential-care facility. But the week before the meeting, Owen, now approaching ninety, suddenly said that he thought that ninety was a good age to take advantage of the convalescent care insurance he had been paying for decades. He was ready. So instead of a confrontational and potentially hurtful session, we were able to use the occasion to assure him of our continuing love and support. The "long good-bye" commenced.

Joan Didion's book *The Year of Magical Thinking* reflects on the sudden death of her husband: "You sit down to dinner . . . And then—gone."[2] Didion describes the shock, the scramble to make the necessary arrangements, the need to cope with sympathy not always expressed in helpful ways, the pain of loss barely understood and emotionally unacceptable that characterized the trauma of her

2. Didion, *Year of Magical Thinking*, 26.

husband's unanticipated death.[3] By contrast, families of dementia patients usually undergo "the long goodbye,"[4] similarly—but in a different way—eviscerating to loved ones.

Every family's experience of dementia is different. At best, perhaps my experience can suggest attitudes and actions that helped me and may be useful to someone else. For example, I learned not to suffer unnecessarily. One day Owen asked me my name saying, "Why have I never seen you before?" He was astonished when I told him that he and I have been married for thirty-four years. These "facts"—my name and the years of our marriage, even memory of our marriage itself—eluded him. But I was convinced that he knew *me*, my presence. Even my name was somewhere in his head; when I arrived unexpectedly at his bedside to visit him, he often exclaimed involuntarily, "Oh Margaret! It's so good to see you!" My name is not me; he knew me, but was sometimes unable to name me.

Another way I found to avoid unnecessary suffering was to distinguish between things that matter and things that don't matter. I found that in stressful times it is difficult to determine whether something that arises to be dealt with *matters*. It helped me to articulate—spell out—my governing values in relation to Owen's disease; then it was possible to identify actions and attitudes that act out these values. My values, and the activities that support them, *matter*.

For example, I valued Owen having the best quality of life that was possible for him; I sought the activities that engaged and pleased him. The limit of this value is the point at which others will be inconvenienced or annoyed by his behavior. Usually, however, he would not enjoy occasions he had formerly enjoyed, but at which he now might be annoying to others. For example, he would become restless and vocal if he had to sit for a long time in

3. Hence *The Year of Magical Thinking*, namely, the "silent thought" that her husband would return and would need his shoes and other belongings, that he was merely in the next room and would reappear at any moment.

4. The title of Raymond Chandler's 1953 novel, written while his wife was terminally ill, subsequently a neo-noir film directed by Robert Altman (1973).

an unfamiliar environment such as a concert, a restaurant, or even a church service. He would be likely to turn to me and say, as he once did in a loud voice at a particularly quiet moment in church, "I need the men's room."

Inevitably, since Owen cannot relate his experience of dementia, it will be my experience, my thoughts and feelings, which are described in this book. These changed dramatically as his dementia progressed. At first, not understanding that Owen "had something," I was irritated and dismayed by his behavior, which had been diagnosed by his first neurologist as "mild cognitive impairment."

I struggled to decide whether I should try to pull him back to responsible adult behavior and relationship, or let him continue to slide further into his private world. I was bewildered, confused by periods in which he was (what I thought of as) "himself," soon followed by more odd or dangerous behavior. Until it became obvious that I could not control or manage troubling behavior, my pattern of struggling to accept and/or manage him continued and increased as his disease advanced.

I was a widow whose husband was still alive. I am also a writer, and I deal with difficult situations by naming and thus externalizing pain. I write to know what I think. For a writer, someone has said, "the only sure cure is to write a book."[5]

> It would probably not be worth the trouble of making books if they fail to teach the author something she hadn't known before, if they didn't lead to unforeseen places, and if they didn't disperse her to a strange and new relation with herself.
>
> —MICHEL FOUCAULT

Sprinkled throughout these chapters are quotations I have been collecting from my eclectic reading for many years. I came upon them in a variety of sources, such as *The New York Times*

5. Saul Bellow, letter to Alice Adams, quoted in Wieseltier, "Saul Bellow's Quest," 13.

Book Review, ancient philosophers, or contemporary novels. Each articulates a thought that has been useful to me—encouraging, enlightening, reminding, or energizing me. In times of anxiety and/or stress, these quotations have comforted and challenged me as needed. Each of them played a role in sustaining me through the long goodbye. They helped!

Is dementia *only* painful and horrible for all who are involved? No. The temptation is to lament, "Why me, Lord?" But as the third-century Platonic philosopher, Plotinus, wrote, the question *should* be "Why not me?" Plotinus taught that the gifts and pains of the universe are not rewards and punishments; they circulate randomly, so why should I not accumulate some of both?

Is dementia sad? Of course it is. Yet I have also found insight, beauty, and richness in the experience of loving a dementia patient. For example, the whole circle of Owen's life was revealed as he became again the little boy I hadn't known. At moments during the dementia decade I learned, I understood, I marveled at beauty. That is what this book is about. When I tell my new friends—family members who regularly visit their loved ones in the dementia unit—that I want to write about the moments of beauty, they are not surprised, agreeing immediately that these moments exist. Each of them could provide further examples of such incidents. But when I tell friends who have *not* experienced loved ones' dementia they are surprised, even shocked at the suggestion that the dread disease could offer any beauty at all. Sometimes they accused me of being "in denial."

How, then, to tell about a decade of my life in a way that acknowledges both the beauty and the pain? How to explore simultaneously the personal and the social dimensions of dementia? I begin by acknowledging that these superficially different dimensions are, in fact, inseparable. Individuality (as uniqueness), is an American myth, foundationally embedded in the story we tell ourselves about our lives. Just as intrepid pioneers settled the American landscape, each of us sees ourselves as a pioneer of our own experience. But we are also profoundly formed and informed by the family, the landscape, the society, and the culture in which we participate. Even dissent from some of the values of our society shapes us. My decade of living with a dementia patient prompted me to seek the unexamined assumptions that lie simultaneously just under the surface of my own thinking and in the public mind of my society. In chapter 2, I explore the cultural and religious myths that provide the deep background of the story I *make* of my experience. In chapter 6, I examine the personal and the social, their interdependence, and their effects in greater detail.

This book does not offer medical advice. Dementia expresses itself differently in different patients, and medical professionals prescribe differently according to different presenting symptoms. Moreover, there is a great deal of medical information and advice on offer; only a small part of it is listed in my bibliography. Internet sites, regularly updated, are a source of information unavailable to earlier generations.

Chapter 2

INTERLUDE: FRAMING THE STORY

> So much depends on how we understand what happened to us . . . So much depends on how we tell ourselves the story of our lives.
>
> —James R. Gaines

Several stories attempt to explain why human beings seem perennially to exhibit asocial behavior. In his fifth-century BCE *History of the Peloponnesian War*, Thucydides wrote, "The strong do what they can, and the weak suffer what they must."[1] According to Thucydides, this situation is simply "the natural order," a law of human nature, warranting neither blame nor praise. Our use of the word "human" reflects the ambiguity of human nature: Excusing someone who has acted badly we say, "Well, he's only human." Yet we also use the word "human" as praise; we speak of a generous person as a human being, a *mensch*.

> It is extremely rare to have a chance to see someone training himself to be a human being.
>
> —Pierre Hadot

1. Thucydides, "Melian Dialogue," in *The History of the Peloponnesian War*.

The third-millennium BCE *Epic of Gilgamesh* narrates the emerging consciousness of the first tragic hero. Gilgamesh, king of Uruk in Mesopotamia, had the desires of a god and the strength of a man. He "went abroad in the world," doing whatever he wanted to do and meeting with no opposition. "No son is left with his father, for Gilgamesh takes them all. . . . His lust leaves no virgin to her lover, neither the warrior's daughter nor the wife of the noble. Yet the king should be a shepherd to his people."[2] To remedy this intolerable situation the gods created Enkidu, a wild man, more animal than human. Enkidu and Gilgamesh each believed himself to be the strongest man in the world, and when they met, they fought. Finally acknowledging that Gilgamesh's strength "surpasses the strength of men," Enkidu accepted defeat and they embraced in friendship.

The Epic of Gilgamesh can be read as the story of every human being. Born both needy and with the illusion of omnipotence, the infant acts as if no one would provide for him unless he loudly demands care and food. He understands no difference between needs and desires. He is the only person in his world; everyone he sees exists to serve him. He insists on bending the world to his will.

Enkidu's strength forced Gilgamesh to respect the boundaries required by another's existence. The infant first learns—or fails to learn—from the primary caregiver, usually his mother, that s/he is not merely an obedient provider, an extension of the infant, but a separate person with her own needs, desires, and limited endurance. Subsequently, the child's playmates provide further experience that others exist, that their desires are as urgent as his, and that his desires must be negotiated with theirs. The child who does not learn this at an early age is likely to have many struggles and bruises before he understands that others exist. Some never learn; they continue to attempt to assert their power over others throughout life. They picture every circumstance as a win or lose situation. At best, they learn to conceal their efforts under a façade of congeniality.

2. *Gilgamesh*, 60.

> What in the end causes a human being to be one way rather than another? What accident of history or temperament makes the difference? What buried childhood memory of cruelty or mercy or kindness? What tender light? What sudden blow from behind? And what, finally, do we know of each other?
>
> —KATHLEEN HILL

A third explanation of antisocial behavior is provided by Christian scripture and tradition, which states that every child is born sinful: "I was a sinner from my mother's womb," wrote the psalmist.[3] "Original sin" names the assumption that the "real" person is rude, destructive, dirty, and aggressive; this is proposed as the "truth" that lies at the heart of being human. St. Augustine saw evidence of original sin when he observed an infant looking jealously at another infant who shared his mother's milk. Nothing but weakness, he said, kept the infant from destroying his caregivers when they did not obey his demands;[4] "I so small a boy and so great a sinner."[5] Older but no wiser, the youthful Augustine, by his own account, still had no boundaries: "no friendship was free of my lust."[6]

However, recent studies of infant behavior challenge Augustine's observation and interpretation, indicating that original sin is "in the eye of the beholder." From an ontogenetic perspective pleasure and openness to another's presence precedes the first evidence of fear of, or aggression toward, the other. Infants smile *intentionally* at about two months. They are not simply imitating the mother's smile; they are experiencing pleasure in the presence of another, for *blind babies smile.* The first antisocial fear-based behavior occurs at about nine months, as "stranger anxiety," a reaction

3. Ps 51.6.
4. *Confessions* 1.7.
5. Ibid., 1.12.
6. Ibid., 3.1.

that much later is extended into xenophobia.[7] It is not, then, "sin" that is ontogenetically original, but pleasure and friendliness.

The Christian doctrine of original sin is not, however, based on Augustine's observation of the "jealous" infant, but on St. Paul's insistence that in some mysterious way, all human beings participate in the sin and the guilt of Adam, progenitor of the human race. In fact, St. Paul's assertion informed Augustine's interpretation of the infant's look, not *vice versa*.

Is a child's "true self" revealed in its most antisocial behavior? Or is the sweetness of the infant's smile and the sweetness that often appears in old age more accurate evidence of the "real self"? My Calvinist mother agreed with Augustine: if I, as a child, was crabby, perhaps with a headache or incipient flu, my mother observed, "That's your real self coming out." In similar circumstances my friend's mother said, "You're not yourself today, dear!" These reactions emerge from profoundly different theories of human nature.

Does dementia offer light on the "true self"? Infants and dementia patients have a great deal in common. Dementia patients revert to childhood, losing boundaries they have respected throughout their adult lives. They urinate in the waste can, sleep in others' beds, and express themselves loudly without considering others' feelings. They do and say what they want, when they want. They do not self-inhibit. They have no filter and, unlike infants, they are unteachable. They are free of boundaries, but in one sense only. They are also locked up, "for their own safety," and told when to eat, shower, sleep, and take a walk. Their personalities may change dramatically, from docile to angry or from irascible to patient. We who love them say that they are not "themselves," that we do not recognize the gentle mother we loved or the husband with whom we shared life. Or, informed by an assumption deeply embedded in Western societies that we are all fundamentally asocial—"selfish"—we may think that the dementia-self represents the emergence of the "real self."

7. Sheets-Johnstone, *Roots of Morality*, 363ff.

The question of whether human beings are *at bottom* good or evil assumes that human nature can be simplified to a fundamental characteristic. *The question itself is wrong.* Both infants and dementia patients exhibit the full range of human feelings and behaviors. "Nothing human is alien to me."[8] Observation can provide anecdotal evidence to defend either view of human nature. Lacking final authorization for either, we must be content to recognize that each of us has enormous potential for good or evil:

> People do not "have" ideas, they "make" them.
>
> —Mary Carruthers

I found that I needed to jettison the "silent thought"—the unarticulated and unexamined assumption—that my experience comes to me already interpreted. "Everyone knows," for example, that dementia is a horrible disease in which the person who has it gradually loses everything, and those who love him lose him. In fact, we don't simply "have" experience. To a much greater extent than we usually recognize, we *make* experience, either by tacitly accepting others' interpretations of similar experience, or by *making our own.* Loving someone with dementia, we are tempted to passivity in the face of rather overwhelming evidence that dementia consists of nothing but horror stories and grief. But the alternatives to this scenario are neither Pollyanna-ish cheeriness nor unrelieved sadness.

It is possible to look *within the situation* to identify resources, with which to *make* my experience. My example comes from the eighth-century CE epic, *Beowulf.* The monster, Grendel, was in the habit of sneaking into the mead hall where Beowulf's soldiers were sleeping it off and snatching several of them for his midnight snack. Beowulf, of course, could not tolerate this and swore to kill Grendel. He took his trusty sword, Hrunting, "which had never failed any man who carried it." But when Beowulf cornered the monster in its den under the sea, "his flashing blade was harmless

8. Terence, "Heauton Timorumenos," Act 1, scene 1.

and would not bite." Beowulf, glancing around desperately, caught a glimpse of "a fine giant sword hanging on a wall." He grabbed the sword, and with it killed Grendel and his defenders.[9] The example is more dramatic than the point it illustrates. The point is that those whose lives are closely entwined with a dementia patient can find tools within our circumstance with which to *make* our experience—experience that is simultaneously shared with many others in similar relationships *and* unique.

> A lively and understandable spirit / Once entertained you. /
> It will come again. / Be still. / Wait.
>
> —Theodore Roethke

It is possible to refuse a "one size fits all" interpretation of the experience of loving someone with dementia, declining a "helpless victim" mentality. I may allow *moments* of collapse into sadness, but I can resist a settled attitude of sorrow over the changes I see in my loved one from day to day. If I succumb to grief, I will not notice opportunities for learning and moments of beauty; these resources are there to be found. With the sword hanging on the wall I can *make* my experience.

Although religious diversity presently characterizes American public life, some ancient Christian "stories of our lives" are often implicit in our attitudes and behavior. Original sin, the conviction that people are fundamentally flawed by an evil urge, seems to have longevity in twenty-first-century American life far beyond conscious belief. Recall, for example, the voyeuristic delight we as a society take in media revelations of the less-than-virtuous actions of public figures. Although we may object to the doctrine of original sin, we routinely assume that the "true self" has been revealed when a secret vice has been brought to light. We are eager to reduce apparent integrity to unacknowledged self-interest; we often think of virtue as little more than a mask for vice.

9. *Beowulf*, 62–64.

This is a social problem; American understandings of poverty, lack of education, and other social problems reveal that we are eager to blame the victims as deserving their distress. But reluctance to tell ourselves a different "story of our lives" is also a personal problem.

My experience of loving a person with dementia required a painful increment of self-knowledge, namely the acknowledgment that underneath my conscious belief in human goodness lay dark suspicions that Owen's frustrating behavior was fueled by deception, stubbornness, and a willful intent to foil the best efforts of those who cared for him. Again and again I had to learn that dementia is a *disease* whose many symptoms are not willfully chosen. Again and again I had to resist my predilection for assuming that the behavior I found so frustrating revealed Owen's "real self." In the struggle to *make* my experience, this difficult and repetitious learning was crucial. "The Sunset Prayer of the Reverend Eli Jenkins," from Dylan Thomas's radio play, *Under Milk Wood*, suggests a different story of human nature from the one I inherited from my particular childhood and from the society in which I grew up.

> Every morning when I wake,
> Dear Lord, a little prayer I make,
> O please to keep Thy lovely eye
> On all poor creatures born to die.
>
> And every evening at sun-down
> I ask a blessing on the town,
> For whether we last the night or no
> I'm sure is always touch-and-go.
>
> We are not wholly bad or good
> Who live our lives under Milk Wood,
> And thou, I know, wilt be the first
> To see our best side, not our worst.

O let us see another day!
Bless us this night, I pray,
And to the sun we all will bow
And say, good-bye—but just for now.[10]

The following chapters describe my experience of loving my husband as dementia gradually but relentlessly took him from me.

10. Thomas, *Under Milk Wood.*

Chapter 3

AT HOME

> Here are the years that walk between, bearing
> Away the fiddles and the flutes, restoring
> One who moves in the time between sleep and waking,
> wearing
> White light folded, sheathed about her, folded.
>
> —T. S. ELIOT

FROM APPROXIMATELY 2005, OWEN began to behave in ways that compromised his relationships outside as well as within the home. Although his behavior was amply documented dementia behavior, most of the people he dealt with had little knowledge of dementia and therefore did not take the disease into account in their reactions to him.

I began to record evidence that Owen was "not himself"—I didn't know how else to name it. I thought vaguely that I should "keep track" of incidents of uncharacteristic behavior in case I might later need to document it. Owen's "mild cognitive impairment," diagnosed in 2006, was increasingly evident every day. He was agitated and impatient; his nervous energy seemed to absorb the air in any room. At dinner at a friend's home he knocked a glass of water off the table; it shattered on the carpet and hardwood floor. At the same friend's home, he clumsily kicked a glass of wine he had set on the floor by his chair, sending it whirling across the room. Incidents like these made me begin to dread going anywhere with him.

I puzzled about what attitude to take with him. Should I try to recall him to thoughtful and meaningful engagement with myself and others, or should I simply detach, distancing myself from his behavior? I always seemed to be anxious, afraid of losing friends, explaining his behavior to myself and others. When I had a choice, I went out without him, but then I felt guilty for excluding him. At home, Owen and I ate dinner together, watched an occasional DVD, and went to church together—that was approximately the sum of our interaction. My journal entries at that time describe my desperate effort to understand what was happening to him. Sometimes I endeavored to make the best of his dementia behavior. For example:

> August 12, 2005
>
> *Dementia is, on one level, fascinating. I can follow the connections in Owen's conversation for a short time, but soon they occur too rapidly. I can't keep up. Our minds have been rendered sluggish by the centuries-long habit of rationality, which slows our thinking considerably. I assume that a person with dementia is "making sense," even if not to me. The connections are there, they are just too rapid for me to track. Released from the habit of rationality we could think much faster. But there is a price to pay. Communication with another person is impossible because the relevant information exists only in the mind of the person speaking.*

Owen's early dementia behavior exaggerated ways he had always acted. He didn't listen to women—now perhaps, although he had state-of-the-art hearing aids, he could not *hear* women's voices. He asked questions that the person with whom he was talking had just answered—perhaps he had heard a word or two, prompting his question. He slapped women on the back, a habit I had tried for years to get him to stop. He cleared his throat incessantly; he broke things, and he bumped his head repeatedly on familiar cupboards, creating bloody sores. In the thirty-five years I had known him he had done these things occasionally; now he did them very frequently. He dropped, spilled, and lost things—glasses, wallet, cell phone, hearing aids. Sometimes—not always—these items were found later.

For several years Owen's sons and I had been urging him to stop driving, but he insisted on continuing to drive. He hit several stationary objects—a parked car, a tree, a large garbage bin behind a grocery store; my daughter nicknamed his car the "red dents." I heard that the Department of Motor Vehicles will test a person and decide whether that person can safely continue to drive. He agreed to take the DMV tests—a driving test, an eye test, and a book test. I thought it a foregone conclusion that he would be told that he should not continue to drive. But he passed all the tests and was told that it was safe for him to drive. I had no grounds on which to contest the DMV decision. However, one day his doctor asked him if he was still driving and, in reply to Owen's affirmative response, said that he shouldn't be. The voice of authority had spoken; the next day Owen went with me to the DMV to "surrender" his license, after which we had lunch to celebrate his many years of accident-free driving.[1]

I urged him many times not to try to do things that either were too difficult and frustrating for him, or that would require a great deal of help from others. Challenged on instances of inappropriate or dangerous behavior, he simply claimed to be "losing my mind." I asked him to think about his age and whether, for example, he should still be playing tennis. He insisted that he could play tennis as he always had; only, he complained, the recent difficulty of finding tennis partners proved insurmountable.

During this time my mother's often repeated question was always in my mind: "What next?" I was sad, lonely, and bewildered.

1. Imagine the unnecessary emotional weight the word "surrender," used in DMV literature, holds for men of Owen's age whose strongest association with the word was World War II.

"Don't leave me," I sobbed, driving in the car by myself one day. But I realized, of course, that he *was* leaving me every day, a little at a time. Watching him my sister observed one day, "You no longer have your companion."

Contributing to my confusion, there were times when Owen was able to manage rather strenuous and complicated activities. In 2011 he attended a professional conference in San Francisco that involved staying for three nights in a hotel and taking taxis to sessions in different locations in the city. He left his wallet in one taxi; otherwise, as far as I know, he managed.

Owen tried the medical remedies on offer. The prescription, Aricept, which had helped others with short-term memory loss, caused him a great deal of discomfort—nausea, diarrhea, loss of sleep, buzzing in his head, and increased agitation. It brought no positive results, so he stopped using it. He also tried Namenda with similar results. These drugs made him so uncomfortable that we resolved together that he would not try other dementia drugs.

Owen's deafness increased. His first tests had revealed hearing loss primarily in the register of *my* voice! By 2006 he no longer conversed because he could not hear what others were saying. In company, he talked and talked so that he didn't need to listen. Due to his poor hearing, misunderstandings occurred—some funny. I told him, "No mail yet." He replied emphatically, "Throw it out!" I said, "Look at the lamp, I jerry-rigged it." "Who's Jerry?" he asked suspiciously. In the chaos of his room he hung his boxer shorts on the knobs of his dresser to stretch them, claiming that they pinched him; layers of his shorts adorned the dresser. Outside the front door, five or six blue sticks (a couple of feet tall) appeared in a planted area. When I asked why they were there, Owen said he put them there to prevent the post person from stepping on the plants. I wrote down for him where I went each day, but often he forgot to refer to the note and called me to see where I was.

For several years Owen suffered from attacks of vertigo which lasted for two or three hours. When these occurred at home he would not, as I urged, simply sit down wherever he was; he insisted on going to his bed. I tried to help him but was not strong enough to keep him upright. We both fell. We fell again on an Oakland street as I was taking him to an appointment with his doctor. I realized that in marrying someone fifteen years older than myself I had tacitly accepted being part of whatever might happen to Owen.

> This is what getting old is all about . . . You get variations of what you need. You go into the world thinking you still know what you want, and the world says: How about considering this instead?
>
> —DENNIS MCFARLAND

As Owen's behavior was becoming increasingly bewildering and consuming to me, I felt a need for distraction, a need to forget for a while, "these matters that with myself I too much discuss, too much explain."[2] I decided to train as a hospice volunteer. In my career as an historian, I had researched, pondered, and written about historical conceptions and practices relating to bodies. Now I wanted to get closer, not to *ideas* about bodies, but to actual living and dying bodies.

Hospice training took six weeks and was largely focused on reassuring a group of frightened but determined people that we could, yes actually *could*, do this work. Trainees had myriad questions about what they should do in hypothetical situations. These questions were usually answered, "Just be yourself," or "Trust your instincts," answers that seemed to me at best frustratingly vague or at worst, worthless clichés. My instincts, I thought, might be more or less adequate to a situation about twenty percent of the time, but what about the other eighty percent? And which of my several "selves" was to be considered trustworthy?

> I've always thought of wholeness and integration as necessary myths. We're fragmented beings who cement ourselves together, but there are always cracks. Living with

2. Eliot, "Ash Wednesday," 109–21.

the cracks is part of being, well, reasonably healthy.

—Siri Hustvedt

There were hospice dos and don'ts. The "hospice handhold" instructed the volunteer to place her hand *under* the patient's so that if the patient didn't want his hand held, he could easily move it. We were, of course, expected to feel compassion for our patient and her family, but we should not become personal friends; we should maintain at all times a small, but respectful, professional distance. When the patient's death was imminent and family members gathered, volunteers were told to back off—literally, to sit in another room unless we were invited to the bedside. When the patient died, "tears may run down your face," we were told, "but you must not sob." Sobbing indicated that our own sorrows were intruding.

As I began to volunteer I learned that no more definitive answers were possible than those that were given in our training. Unpredictable situations arose frequently in which volunteers must "wing it," depending on our ability to be aware and to respond—"just be yourself." In fact, hospice volunteering was simply an extension and intensification of life's general unpredictability and frequent demands.

April 20, 2010

This afternoon I listened to Mozart's Requiem. For the first time I think I understood the meaning of peccatum mundi, *usually translated "sin of the world."* Peccatum mundi *is the strong undertow of the long sadness that lies just under daily life; it is more like* vitium *(weakness) than* peccatum *(sin). Augustine's word* pondeus, *weight,*[3] *also describes* "lacrimae rerum," *the "[tears] sadness of things,"*[4] *a lingering spiritual weight like heavy humidity that is felt even on the happiest occasions. Paul Henry*

3. Augustine, *Confessions* 13.9.

4. Hellenga, *Confessions of Frances Godwin*, 63.

has written, "Wrongdoing is not so much rebellion and defiance as bewilderment and weariness."[5]

Hospice volunteering was full of opportunities to learn, to "get over myself," and to be playful. Volunteers receive as much as we give. We have heard this and said it ourselves so often that it has become a truism. How does it actually work? There are, of course, the rich lives we hear about from our patients and our own very gratifying sense of passing on the attentiveness and caring we have received from others. But there are other, more subtle ways in which we receive as much as we give.

Learning is one of the great pleasures of life. As adults, however, most of us carefully remain within our own areas of knowledge and expertise. Hospice volunteering pushes us to fundamentally new learning. It was a challenge to find the music, the activity, or the conversation that could enhance that patient's precious day. On the other hand, volunteers are released from the demands we impose on ourselves as we begin to recognize that it is not so much what we do or say, but *being there*, that matters. We also benefit from familiarization with death as a part of life, soothing our fears of our own death.

Moreover, in hospice volunteering, we learn to *hold together* some apparent contradictions. Consider, for example, the advice to "Just be yourself." Good advice, but intimacy with strangers also requires the opposite: "Get over yourself." Both injunctions are wise, and the apparent contradiction can be resolved only "on location," in being *with* the patient. I became "more myself" when I recognized that my patient and I both participate conditionally and temporarily in life; I am also a dying person and she is a living person. She has lived in the part of the lifecycle that I presently inhabit, and, I will someday be where she is now. The boundaries between my "self" and her "self" soften a bit and become permeable.

Ellen, who was seventy-nine, had breast cancer and dementia. She was my first hospice patient. Ellen was an artist. Her apartment was filled with beautiful artworks—mostly paintings and

5. Henry, "Introduction," in MacKenna, xxxvi.

collages. I thought that her art would be my way to relate to her; I would ask her to talk about it. But, beyond telling me about her training in various techniques and media, she didn't want to talk about it. Rather, she wanted to talk about *teaching* art. She told me that her students often came into the Jewish Center saying, "I'm not going to be able to do this, Mrs. G." And she would tell them, "Oh yes you can." "And they *could*," she always concluded triumphantly.

People who are near death are often playful. They can let go of the preoccupations, fears, and projects that had defined them and prevented spontaneity. Ellen and I discovered that we both loved to listen to classical music. One day as we listened to a CD, Ellen began gently to conduct the music. I did too, and we gestured more and more wildly, dancing while sitting down, laughing. One day we fantasized that we were ladies in beautiful dresses, listening to music in one of the great concert halls of the world. We imagined the dresses, their design, their colors, and the diamonds that dripped from our necks and ears. She said to me once, "None of my other friends will sit quietly and listen to music with me." And of course, under "normal" circumstances, one doesn't visit a friend in order to sit quietly listening to music. The proximity of death often frees both the "dying" person and her visitor to a broader range of activities than is permitted by polite social behavior. I brought art books, and we looked at them together. Ellen studied them attentively and talked to me about what worked and what didn't work in the paintings. Her highest praise for a painting was "*That* took some doing!" Ellen died in her sleep several months after I first visited her.

Hospice volunteering offers the possibility of life-changing awareness of a larger universe than the one we inhabit as socialized, practical, isolated selves. It produces an awareness of the reality of life and death. It intensifies and makes vivid the life we share—all of us living and dying, dying and living people—with our patients and our loved ones for a bit longer.

April 4, 2010

On Good Friday Owen "heard" confessions in the side chapel at the Episcopal church where he was affiliated clergy. But, of course, he couldn't hear well, so he asked the person confessing to speak loudly and more slowly. But the last thing a person making a painful confession wants to do is to speak loudly and slowly; they desperately want to speak rapidly and softly! A friend remarked that the image of a hearing-challenged person "hearing" confessions is theologically beautiful. The confessor doesn't hear and thus does not need to struggle not to think less of the "miserable miscreant," but can nevertheless assure the penitent of God's love and forgiveness.

Other incidents involving Owen's clergy status were less benign. Owen (age 88) told me that he had been accused of propositioning women at church. This is a very serious infraction of the behavior required of a priest. He told me that "the last two" women he propositioned were very angry, his puzzled tone implying that he thought that these women should have been flattered. One of the women went directly to the diocesan bishop, by-passing the interim rector. The bishop withdrew Owen's clergy license and required that he never again "set foot in" that church.

I explained to the interim rector that Owen had been diagnosed with cognitive impairment four years ago and that his recent actions were textbook dementia behavior. He expressed surprise, saying that dementia had not occurred to him, and that he would explain this to the woman who had complained to the bishop. He added that he *hoped* that this explanation would end the complaint so that it would not proceed to a civil lawsuit.

Again I asked myself, is this my personal problem or is it a social problem? Loving a person with dementia is certainly a personal problem, but it is also a social problem in that it often creates painful misunderstandings. With large numbers of baby boomers reaching dementia years, we as a society need to understand dementia better, as Owen's neurologist had said. Had I known more about dementia at the time, I would not have felt as betrayed, hurt, and saddened by Owen's behavior as I did. A friend told me that no fewer than five women had come forward to complain that Owen had spoken to them "inappropriately." If these women had known more about dementia, they would not have felt as personally affronted and victimized as they did. So I determined to address Owen's dementia as a social problem. I wrote to the Episcopal Bishop of California to urge that education be undertaken in the aging congregations of Episcopal churches. I wrote, "A great deal of pain to victims and bystanders could be alleviated by information about the symptoms and likely behaviors of dementia patients. Churches have the communication skills and formats for addressing, and thus preventing, the pain to all concerned caused by common, well documented, dementia symptoms and behavior. There are experts on the topic who can inform and educate clergy and congregations about dementia."

My letter received no response.

I was puzzled by Owen's evident lack of remorse or feelings of any sort in relation to these incidents. He merely grumbled that the whole thing was "overstated." Dementia had already put him in a world of his own, removed from thoughts and feelings he would have had under other circumstances. But this was not the end of the problem. Several months later, Owen received a letter from the interim rector telling him to stop calling a woman he had continued to contact, and threatening a civil suit if he did not. Since Owen claimed to have no memory of his actions, I was fearful that he would continue to contact/harass the woman. I imagined that civil courts have even less tolerance for dementia-prompted behavior than do churches.

However, the behavior eventually stopped. Owen went to Brazil to visit his youngest son and his family for a month. This entailed a complicated flight with several plane changes (assisted by an airport concierge) which Owen was able to manage. His ability to accomplish a complex trip seemed incompatible with his inability to understand the seriousness of his behavior at home. On his return, I asked him if he would be happier living with his son's family in Brazil, a large, busy extended family in which there is always something going on. I thought that living with a family in which several people could share his care might mean that he would not need to live in a care facility. He was not intrigued by the suggestion, nor, apparently, was his son's family.

For many men of Owen's generation, World War II and pursuit of women were occasions of the feelings of greatest aliveness and intensity of their lives. During World War II, Owen, then a doctoral student in physics at Cornell University, was recruited to work in a naval laboratory in Washington, DC. Many of his friends, however, fought, killed, and were killed in the war. In the intervening years, Owen never missed an opportunity to view old movies about the war, even if for the fourteenth time. They still carried a "contact high" for him decades later.

Trying to understand with generosity, I speculated that when a man of his generation experiences both the end of his career and the ebbing of his sexual attractiveness, he might well seek to feel alive in the only way available to him, namely by pursuing women. Both the women he met at church and several of my dearest friends became unwilling victims of Owen's desperate search for *more life*.

> We beg you, make us truly alive.
>
> —Serapion of Thmuis, ancient eucharistic prayer

August 26, 2010

The frequency of "incidents" related to Owen's dementia increased. Owen lost his glasses (which turned up mysteriously on the driveway, run over); hearing aids were repeatedly lost and sometimes found, and his wallet was lost and not found. He dropped a glass of ouzo while placing it on the table. Attempting to catch it he kicked it as it fell—a soccer instinct, I suppose—spraying sticky liquid across the room.

On Easter Sunday 2011, sitting in church before the service, Owen felt cold. He asked the usher to close the church doors, but the usher said that the church doors must be open while people were coming and going. So Owen tied his wool neck scarf around his ankles. It looked so funny. He accused me of laughing at his "pain"; I said no, I was laughing at *him*, affectionate laughter, he knew that.

> July 11, 2011
>
> *Mistakes of judgment occurred regularly; he gave the phone number of a young couple to a man who regularly asked members of the congregation for money. When I talked to him about the inappropriateness of this, he claimed again that he was "losing my mind."*

Again I urged him not to try to do things that have become too difficult for him. I said that "aging gracefully" includes figuring out, and declining, to do things that promise to be too frustrating, too difficult, or will require too much help from others. This mini-lecture had no discernible effect on him.

Chapter 4

TRANSITION TO ASSISTED LIVING

Learn to understand yourself and take pity on yourself.

—St. Teresa of Ávila

Owen struggled on, losing things, forgetting things. He was still at home, but I was finding it more and more difficult to maintain a façade of normalcy. I welcomed his plans to visit his youngest son and family in Brazil for a month. This would be time out for me! I would begin a writing project, which I had been unable to do; my "brain space" had been occupied with anxiety and the daily distraction of Owen's needs.

January 18, 2012

Owen was to go to Brazilia today. We arrived at the San Francisco airport on time for his flight. I had been unable to get a boarding pass on my computer, so we lined up to get one, but were told that a visa is necessary for going to Brazil. Owen had gone to Brazil to visit his son three times in the past decade, so his travel agent assumed that Owen knew he needed a visa. But he had forgotten. So, at first I asked cheerfully, "All right, so at which desk can we get a visa?" Slowly the realization dawned that he couldn't—and wouldn't—be going. Getting a visa is complicated and takes weeks. The trip to Brazil had to be postponed until February, allowing time to get a visa. I realized that in future I must take responsibility for everything requiring hearing and memory.

February 15, 2012

Attempting to think of outings that Owen might enjoy in the meantime, I took him to see the "Red Oak Victory," a WWII battleship docked in the Richmond Point harbor. At the freeway exit, Owen insisted that we should turn east. We went several miles away from the ocean and toward Sacramento before finally stopping to get directions. We should have turned west. Still, we had some luck. We arrived at the Red Oak Victory at 2:00, just as the last tour of the day on the ship was starting. Owen loved it, especially the old radar equipment, which he had worked on during the war. We visited another WWII ship, the SS Missouri, later in the Spring.

February 22, 2012

Owen arrived safely in Brazil. When he left on the airport shuttle, I went back into the house, shut the door, and lay down on the couch. I slept, exhausted, for a half hour. Then I got up and started cleaning the house; I don't have much incentive to do this when he's here because there will inevitably, and quite soon, be spills and messes. I determined to use this time by myself to get away from the fearful state of mind in which I've been living—constantly thinking, "what next, what next?" I know that something worrying is going to happen at any moment, but I don't know what it will be, or how to prevent it. Today the day stretches out invitingly before me. I could do almost anything, go almost anywhere! I have a feeling of freedom and freshness. I am already dreading the end of this time. Can I do better with Owen? Can I do better with myself while living with him? In Brazil Owen continued to lose things—a hearing aid, his glasses, and his plane ticket, found by his son in his carry-on bag.

April 3, 2012

I must take over the household finances. While he was away I paid several of Owen's overdue bills, and reviewing our monthly expenses I found several large mistakes. I had been reluctant to deal with finances so I ignored evidence that he should not be doing them any longer.

April 5, 2012

I wondered whether there are resources in the community for dealing with dementia that I should know and could use. I did some research and invited a case worker from the local Senior Center to visit us. A young man came; he had ridden his bicycle up the long hill to our home and was sweating profusely. His only advice was that Owen should not be driving. This advice was not taken, and I admit to some relief that it was not, because if Owen couldn't drive, I would need to drive him everywhere. That very evening, for example, he had a dinner meeting that would take three hours. He drove.

The possibility that I could work on writing projects that required not only time but also "brain space" seemed more and more remote. Space for thinking seems impossible when I am living in anxiety and dealing with the unpredictable consequences of Owen's behavior. I also feared that since I had declined several lecture and publication invitations, I would not continue to be invited.

June 6, 2013

Our thirty-third wedding anniversary; Owen has always called June 6 "D-Day."; today he did not associate any meaning at all with the date. I made sandwiches and took him for a picnic to the Berkeley Rose Garden, where he used to play tennis. I showed him our wedding pictures and talked about our wedding, hoping to prime his memory, but when I asked him if he remembered it, he said he remembered nothing.

I arranged for us to have lunch and a tour of The Berkshire, a retirement residence in Berkeley, California. The Berkshire is a very nice place; with insurance, he can afford it. My first thought on entering the studio apartment we were shown was, "I could enjoy living here!" When we departed, Owen remarked only that the residents he met were "boring." To my surprise, and some chagrin, we were told that if/when he lives there, Owen could keep and use his car. Clearly, I was highly ambivalent about the alternatives: Owen driving, or driving Owen?

June 9, 2013

Owen is depressed about his life. He says that he has been a failure in everything—as a husband, a father, and professionally—a thought that is patently untrue. He gathers evidence to support his feeling of professional failure from as long ago as his contested tenure review. Tenure reviews are always contested, but he was granted tenure. I told him that his depression is caused by dementia, that he should consciously recall and treasure counterevidence to his feeling of failure. On our anniversary two days ago we had remembered with pleasure many good times together—sabbaticals in Rome, vacations at beautiful beaches, houses in which we have been happy, publication parties for our books, and his retirement dinner. I recall that my father, in old age, also found it difficult to remember the good times, and all too easy to recall in vivid detail his "failures." I tried to convince Owen that perhaps, at this point in life, the "failures" should be forgotten, since nothing can be done about them!

We decided that The Berkshire was a good place for Owen. But there were problems. Would he be accepted? We didn't hear for several days, and I was told that he had said "something inappropriate" to the young female director of admissions. At this time I was not so sure that he was unable to prevent this behavior; after all, he had never, to my knowledge, propositioned lesbians or married women. By now very tired of these episodes of "inappropriate" behavior, I told him that I would leave him if he was rejected.

But Owen was accepted and moved to The Berkshire on July 9, 2012. His needs were evaluated and he was placed in the Independent Living unit. He showered in his own bathroom, toileted and dressed himself, and managed his own medications. His room included a small kitchen with a microwave and refrigerator. He had meals in the communal dining room where food choices were provided. Although he would be required to sign himself out and back in when he left the Berkshire, he could come and go as he pleased.

I attempted to supply Owen with everything he needed to feel that he was still in charge of his own life, still able to spend his days as he usually did—a computer, a cell phone, a television, and a turntable (so that he could play his Benny Goodman records, though I think he never did). I bought him an easy chair and a bed and brought his small desk from home. At his request I also brought him a bottle of Campari and nuts so that he could host a social hour for a few of his new friends before dinner. However, he quickly found that alcohol interfered with many prescriptions and thus was forbidden to most of the residents. The pleasure of a drink before dinner was also undermined by the requirement that the bottle be kept at the medicine desk, and the drink measured and dispensed as if it were a prescription. Owen complained that the staff treated him like a child. He thought that if he wore his professional clothes he would be treated with respect as a professor. Because he spilled food on himself with nearly every bite, cleaning bills were high.

Owen's ninetieth birthday arrived to be celebrated. He and I went on a brunch cruise in the San Francisco Bay. The brunch was lavish, and Owen enjoyed exploring the large ship. The ship passed *under* the Golden Gate Bridge, offering a view of the bridge that we had never before seen! But family members in the vicinity also wanted to celebrate Owen's birthday, so I planned a birthday dinner and invited his son and Owen's Berkshire "special friend," Dorothy. Staff told me that she could not be considered a "consenting adult," so I called her guardian to ask permission for her to come. Owen's granddaughter, Nina, visiting from Brazil, had prepared two picture boards of snapshots that showed Owen from infancy to young adulthood and on to professor, priest, and the present—Owen sitting in the sunshine on the deck of our home. Nina had also prepared a video in which his two Brazilian great grandchildren sang happy birthday to him in English and Portuguese. The dinner was a celebration of his long and fruitful life.

After dinner Owen's son, Addie, took Dorothy and Owen back to The Berkshire. The director called me the next day to tell me about the events that followed their return. Owen and Dorothy went to Owen's room. When a staff person came looking for Dorothy, Owen came to the door and said that she was not there. But Dorothy could be heard mumbling and humming to herself (as she does most of the time) in the background. Staff are not permitted to force locks, so when persuasion failed, police were called to break into the room and extricate Dorothy.

I imagined that Owen was feeling (what Camus has called) the "mortal cold of the universe." I told a friend this; she replied, "Did he tell you this?" "No," I admitted. "Well," she said, "I think you are projecting from what you imagine *you* would feel in a similar circumstance." Perhaps she was right, but his behavior did suggest to me that he was feeling bleak and alone.

September 6, 2012

Owen worried that he would be unable to find his doctor's office where he had an appointment the next day. So he got up about 3:00 a.m. and drove to the office. When he arrived back at The Berkshire, he found the doors locked. So he went around to all the ground floor windows, knocking loudly. He could not get anyone to open the door, so he called the police, who called a Berkshire administrator, who came and opened the door. The next day I complained to the director that since people with dementia are known to wander, there should be a person who watches the door at night.

It was not to be Owen's last episode of wandering.

> The questions are not, what did I do wrong, and how should I have done differently? They are, why did he persist in things that didn't work and why would he not go for help or accept it when it was offered? These questions are unanswerable, of course, but then so were the original ones.
>
> —Sue Chance

Frequently discouraged, and sometimes overwhelmed with sadness and frustration, I endeavored to make a life for myself with the help of friends, writing projects, and hospice volunteering. This endeavor was complicated by the necessity of dealing, on emotional and practical levels, with my adult son's alcoholism.

As I finished graduate school in 1977 and began teaching at Harvard, Ric finished *with* college. He did not graduate. After four years his basketball scholarship expired, and he had not fulfilled the general education requirements. He had no goals and was not seeking a job. During this time he was on the West Coast and I was on the East Coast. I was working hard and anxiously in those first years of my career. I largely ignored what he was—or wasn't—doing. I had trusted my teenaged children to make their own choices;

my daughter had done well with this strategy. Ric didn't. At present he has had substance abuse problems, mainly alcohol, for over thirty-five years.

I attempted to help, struggling to find the words that would convince Ric to stop drinking. It took me years to figure out that there *is* no right thing, that nothing I might say would produce the hoped-for results. In the first decade after his twenty-first birthday, I borrowed money to pay for three month-long detox and rehab programs. Ric was willing to take a vacation from his harsh life during these times, but the treatment programs were my idea—not his—so of course they didn't work. In 1993 he told me that he suffered from depression, medicating with alcohol and street drugs. I found a psychiatrist who could help. Sometime later the psychiatrist called to tell me that he thought I should know that most of what I was paying for was missed appointments.

> Benevolence is good, but when is it a moral mistake?
>
> —Iris Murdoch

On the advice of a therapist consulted by Ric's parents and step-parents, I agreed to give Ric a social-security-equivalent income. I hoped that this would provide a base—food and shelter—on which he could live while seeking employment. I also benefitted; I was able to concentrate on my difficult and demanding job, which I could not do if Ric were homeless. I sent him (what I thought of as) money for groceries and rent. Soon, however, he was not paying his rent, and I was forced to realize that the money I sent was largely spent on beer. On one occasion he had a psychotic break, screaming and throwing things out of his trailer home; neighbors called police and he was taken to a psychiatric ward for several days. This episode frightened him, and he declared that he would stop drinking. My seemingly endless cycle of hope and despair leaped ahead to hope, only soon to advance to despair; his determination was short lived.

Ric's only transportation was his bicycle. In a decade or so he wore out five bicycles. Once he was in jail for a weekend for drunk driving—on his bike. Several times he had accidents in which he fell and scraped his face on the cement sidewalk.

Fourteen years after agreeing to provide a social-security-equivalent income, his father and I acknowledged that this plan was not working. In order to minimize his temptation to buy beer I agreed to buy him groceries every other week. Beyond the groceries I bought him, he would receive only $10 a week for spending money. This plan proved unsustainable, partly because Ric lived at a distance from me, an hour's drive each way.

May 19, 2008

Ric told me that he wanted to kill himself but he didn't know how. Often I think of Ric as utterly alone, lonely, and longing for me to be his tender, unconditionally loving mother. At other times I think that I represent all that is most dangerous for him—dependence, sympathy, and love that does not require him to grow up, to become self-sufficient. Surely, both are accurate views of Ric.

There is no anguish like the anguish of not being able to make a loved one become the person you think he ought to be.

—LEE SMITH

In 2013 I realized that I would soon have collapsed if both Ric and Owen were "on the front burner," as a friend put it. In addition to Owen's problems, I was exhausted by frequent calls from Ric when he needed money. By now I had had such calls on a more-or-less regular basis for thirty-five years—since he was twenty-one. By chance I heard of an independent case worker, John, who knows the resources of the San Francisco Bay area very well. I hadn't known that such a person existed. I called him, explained Ric's situation, and asked for his help. He described his fees, which seemed to me a small price to pay for my sanity. I retain him to this day.

There is, however, a fundamental problem that limits what John can do for Ric. None of the resources—shelters and programs of various sorts—admits residents who are using alcohol or drugs. John has placed Ric in the best agencies in the area; Ric cooperates for two weeks or so, seems to be doing well, even appears to be pleased with himself; then he suddenly leaves, or drinks and is expelled. I had hoped that with John's help and encouragement, Ric would stop drinking, complete a training program, and be helped to find a job. Alas, like Ric's family, John has found that he cannot do more than attempt to keep Ric alive. John has a limited amount of my money for providing food or the shelter of a cheap motel for Ric when John thinks it wise. I have every confidence that John has more wisdom than I do on the subject.

I am very grateful that the option of putting someone else in charge of Ric's maintenance appeared when I desperately needed it. My own family of origin did not recognize, and thus did not inculcate in me, the necessity of good "self-care." My parents labeled anything resembling self-care "selfishness." My sisters and I, with our gendered socialization, were expected to take care of everyone in sight. The mantra of the fundamentalist Christians who raised me, "I will, with God's help," effectively cancelled human limitation by appropriating omnipotent power. To say, "I can't" was to deny the reality of God's help and was considered a huge failing for a Christian. However, I have learned the redemptive wisdom of recognizing and acknowledging that *I can't* on quite a few occasions in my life. I am grateful that I recognized that being responsible for *two* loved ones "on the front burner" was too much for me. They were still both "on the stove," but I chose to attend primarily to Owen's care in his extreme old age, and to provide for Ric by paying someone who understands his disease.

September 16, 2009

Yesterday I had a helpful talk with a friend. I told her that I was worried about Ric's reaction to what I have written about him. Yes, my honest friend said, "Ric is a bully, and you taught him to be a bully by letting yourself be frightened by his anger. Of course you will write about such a big part of your life. Just tell him, 'You knew I was a writer when you acted like that!'"

September 4, 2012

Old age inevitably involves the cruel stripping away of long-established abilities and accomplishments. Owen had worked very hard on a manuscript of collected writings on Søren Kierkegaard by a deceased mentor of Owen's. He traveled to an archive in Texas where the mentor's writings are collected, wrote a lengthy introduction, and sent a proposal to a publisher. The publisher issued a contract on the strength of his proposal, but the contract depended, as all contracts do, on the submission of a "publishable manuscript." When he submitted the manuscript the editor told him that the manuscript was "a mess," and withdrew the contract. Apparently undaunted, Owen hired a doctoral student to organize and revise the manuscript. This effort did not result in an acceptable manuscript, a sad ending to a fruitful career in academic publishing. In his mind, Owen did not give up on the project. In his last year he showed me the rejected manuscript several times, remarking happily, "I am going to publish this." Fortunately, he had published other books that will continue to attract readers. His students will continue to hear his "voice," especially in his Introduction to Theology, which continues to be helpful to ministerial students for their General Ordination examinations.

People disappear when they die. Their voice, their laughter, the warmth of their breath. Their flesh. Eventually their bones. All living memory of them ceases. This is both dreadful and natural. Yet for some there is

> an exception to this annihilation. For in the books they write they continue to exist. We can rediscover them. Their humor, their tone of voice, their moods. Through the written word they can anger you or make you happy. They can comfort you. They can perplex you. They can alter you. All this, even though they are dead. Like flies in amber, like corpses frozen in ice, that which according to the laws of nature should pass away is, by the miracle of ink on paper, preserved. It is a kind of magic.[1]

Shortly after entering The Berkshire Owen volunteered to give a lecture to the residents on science and religion. The day after he gave it I asked him how it went, expecting his usual, "very well." But he said, "not very well." People complained that he spoke too fast and too loud. Trying to be comforting I said, "It was the wrong audience." He replied, "Probably some of both."

To prevent such painful experiences, a person must decline invitations to continue a range of tasks that he has done well in the past *before* he becomes incapable of doing them well. But dementia rendered Owen unable to evaluate his abilities. A hidden benefit of dementia—there should be one!—is that he had little or no memory of incidents, whether joyous or painful, and thus did not appear to suffer.

> One must feel the washing of the tide over all that has been so meticulously etched by hand.
>
> —JOYCE SCHULD

Owen's transition to residence in The Berkshire entailed many new tasks for me—from buying furniture for his room, to money management. But it also held the hope that my life would henceforth be calmer and that I would have better ability to concentrate. With dear friends in the area, I thought that I would not be lonely and that surely I would not miss Owen as he was. I looked forward to not cooking, or cooking only for myself—a yogurt or popcorn for

1. Setterfield, *Thirteenth Tale*, 138.

dinner! I looked forward to not having sticky counters and floors from frequent spills.

I did miss him, though—perhaps not the Owen of recent days, but my companion of earlier years. At first I visited him every other day for a couple of hours, later increasing my visits to every day for several hours—or as long as I could endure. Often I drove home in tears of anguish that our marriage had come to this. Not yet able to find *within* the circumstances resources with which to make this experience *mine,* I felt desolate. My inner voice chided me for not being more resourceful, but I was too overwhelmed by this huge life change to accept it simply as challenge. That took several months and "a little help from my friends," as the Beatles' song says.

Chapter 5

LONG WALK HOME

> Life will break you. Nobody can protect you from that, and living alone won't either, for solitude will also break you with its yearning. You have to love. You have to feel. It is the reason you are here on earth. You are here to risk your heart. You are here to be swallowed up. And when it happens that you are broken, or betrayed, or left, or hurt, or death brushes near, let yourself sit by an apple tree and listen to the apples falling all around you in heaps, wasting their sweetness. Tell yourself that you tasted as many as you could.
>
> —Louise Erdrich

As time went by, Owen retreated further and further into childhood. I thought of him as a very young child who needed my protection and care as my little children had needed it long ago. A year or so before he died I saw him as a little boy; I enjoyed seeing the little boy I had never known. His delight in feeding the seagulls, for example, was lovely to see. Six months before he died he became an infant—albeit an infant who could walk and talk. He even slept across the bed as infants often do; his feet hanging over the edge, their weight pulling him down, causing him to fall.

I felt alone. My companion of many years was gone. Two quotations describe my acceptance of being *by myself* in the last year of Owen's life. In Arthur Miller's play *The Misfits*, the Marilyn Monroe character has come to Nevada to establish the required residence for getting a divorce. She is walking up a long flight of steps to the courthouse when her estranged husband suddenly appears. He has flown there to try to stop the divorce proceedings, to beg her to return to him. She refuses, saying, "If I'm going to be alone, I want to be *by myself*."

The second quotation is from Hannah Arendt's book *Thinking*.[1] Arendt writes, "When Socrates goes home he is not alone, he is *by himself*." I had to learn to be—not alone—but "by myself." The word "alone" implies that another, or others, are missing and being missed; it connotes a vacancy, an empty space. The state of being "by myself," by contrast, suggests a *presence*, a privilege, a concentrated wealth, an ability to live in my *whole* life, not only in the midst of my present constraints. When I am by myself I think, and there is a sense in which I am not alone, for thinking is dialectical, a silent dialogue between me and myself. "*Solitude* is that human situation in which I *keep myself company*."[2]

A great deal depends on how we *make* our experience. Owen's dementia made me alone, but I chose to be *by myself*. As Plotinus put it, human life consists of chance and choice; we *choose* what we *make* of the chance that comes to us. As to chance: we get only what life gives us, not what we demand, earn, or (think we) deserve. And as Owen used to say when I was fretting about whether a meal I had prepared for guests was sufficient, the guests were "lucky to get anything!"

My journals evolved from keeping a record of Owen's confusion and misdeeds into keeping track of *myself* against being overwhelmed and collapsing into the horror stories of dementia. They helped me to remember myself, to continue, like Beowulf, to look for the "fine sword" on the wall with which to create my

1. Arendt, *Life of the Mind*, vol. 1, *Thinking*, 185, my emphasis.

2. Ibid., 187.

own experience—simultaneously personal and social—of loving someone with dementia.

> April 2, 2013
>
> *It was dark and I was asleep this morning about six a.m. when I thought I heard the doorbell ring. I decided sleepily that it must have been a dream and tried to return to sleep. But as I was drifting off there was a loud pounding on the door. Frightened, I crept as soundlessly as I could down the stairs and toward the front door. Along the way I realized that murderers and burglars do not usually pound on the front door for admission. That thought helped a bit. I turned on no lights, so that I couldn't be seen from outside. When I got to the door I saw Owen with his walker. He had walked five miles home, mostly uphill, in the dark. The rubber sleeves covering the rear legs of the walker had worn down so that, by the time he arrived at the front door, the legs of the walker without wheels were shrieking—metal on the concrete sidewalk. I opened the door. His first words were, "That was really a stupid thing to do." I agreed. I called the Berkshire to let them know that he was safe and tried to put him to bed, but he was excited and agitated. So I made breakfast for him. Later in the morning I took him to his dentist appointment, then I returned him to the Berkshire. There he told his tale and his caregivers and fellow residents were amazed and full of admiration that he had accomplished the long trek home by himself, in the dark. Enjoying their congratulations, he became rather proud of himself. But he also said that he would never do it again—and he didn't.*

That was Owen: stubborn, physically strong, determined, desperate, wanting home, wanting *more life*.

July 8, 2013

Owen has been at the Berkshire for a year. Sunday as I was taking him "home" after church, he suddenly turned to me and said that he felt that he would not live much longer and he wanted me to know that he loved me very much. He said that he had no physical ailments, only a premonition that he doesn't have long to live. He said, "Thank you for marrying me and for all you have done and do for me." "At the end," he said, "keep it simple."

I was crying too hard to say anything, so the next day I wrote him the following letter:

Dear Owen,

I need to write my thoughts to you because when we talk about real and important things, I cry and can't say what I think and feel. This happened yesterday, after church, when you told me that you expect to die before long. I lost it, unable to bear to think of you dying. So now I will try to say what I wanted to say yesterday, and could not.

I love you very much and miss living with you greatly. It has been and is a huge adjustment for me to live alone. I miss "us"—perhaps not so much us as we were in the last couple of years, but the long "us" that we were for many years before. You have been at the Berkshire for a year this week, and it has been a long, lonely, and sometimes panicky year for me, and I know that it has been very difficult for you.

I appreciate many things about our more than thirty years together. For example, I appreciate enormously your lack of professional jealousy. You never begrudged me the opportunities that came to me. You let me do my work. You even praised me for it repeatedly over the years. This generosity of yours made everything I have managed to do professionally possible, and I am deeply grateful for it. From the beginning of our relationship you made me feel safe in an academic world that was all new and quite frightening to me. We also travelled well together and have had some wonderful times: in Greece, in Rome, at Bellagio and elsewhere in Italy, in Soviet Armenia, on the Cape, in New York City . . . We had a very rich life together. We also had, and have, wonderful friends who offered us opportunities we would not otherwise have had.

I know that we have been disappointing to each other in ways that need not be spelled out here, when I am trying to tell you how I appreciate and love you. The future is unknowable, but we will help each other as much as we can, now and with whatever comes in the future. The future doesn't look rosy to me so I try to stay in the day there is and enjoy its beauty.

So, although it was impossible yesterday to say these things through tears, I hope that you will hear them now. I love you very much and will be with you "for as long as we both shall live."

Margaret

July 20, 2013

Last evening as I was reading in bed, a call came from the Berkshire; Owen had fallen and was in an ambulance on his way to the emergency room. I met him there. By 1:30 a.m. multiple tests had revealed no complications so I took him back to the Berkshire, finally returning to my bed about 2:30.

When a fall involves a head injury, caregivers at The Berkshire are required to send the resident to the emergency room. Owen's falls usually involved head injuries along with various cuts and bruises; several of his falls caused brain hematomas that were very slowly reabsorbed—until the next fall caused another brain bleed. He could not be persuaded to move more slowly and to *always* use his walker. Shortly after his ninetieth birthday, Owen fell and was taken to the emergency room with a large hematoma on his tongue; both arms were heavily bruised. The emergency room doctor thought that he might have cancer; he was referred to an oncologist who ran multiple tests but found no cancer.

On one of our trips to the emergency room, a doctor told me that the only sure way to keep Owen from falling was to place him in a nursing facility in bed, sedated, and restrained. His sons and I agreed that this scenario offered a very poor quality of life, and we did not agree to it, recognizing that we must, then, expect frequent falls. Owen could not be watched every minute, day and night. Hiring a "sitter" was an alternative and I did this briefly. Ultimately, however, I knew that it made no sense unless we hired sitters twenty-four hours a day, seven days a week, for Owen did not fall at predictable times. I felt a huge sadness, realizing that I could not simultaneously keep him safe *and* provide for him an acceptable quality of life.

How could his risk for falling be minimized? I hired a physical therapist to train him in safety measures. In the session I observed, Patrick showed him repeatedly how to stand from sitting with the brake on the walker, and then to take the brake off and walk with the walker. While Patrick was there, Owen obediently tried, but the minute Patrick left, he instantly forgot—or ignored—his instructions. Two weeks later Patrick called me to say that he was terminating Owen's physical therapy because he saw no evidence that he remembered or practiced what he was taught. I had to agree, but I was also despondent because physical therapy was my last hope for reducing his falls. Why can't—or won't—he remember instructions which, I told him repeatedly, were for his safety? My first instinct was to think him stubborn, belligerently insisting on doing things *his way*, his "real self" emerging; the lurking "original sin" thesis raised its ugly head. But then I got over myself sufficiently to remember that he had dementia. He didn't remember *anything*; why should I expect him to remember new ways of moving that revise the way he has moved for over ninety years?

October 13, 2013

John, Ric's case worker, called to tell me that he had taken Ric to the emergency room of San Francisco General Hospital, where he was put on seventy-two hour suicide watch. He said that Ric had not only suicide "ideation" but a plan. Seventy-two hours was the maximum time that he could remain in the hospital under watch.

About this time a dear friend scolded me for not taking better care of myself (by going to visit her). She accused me of being "selfless"—from her, not a compliment! I said that sometimes life simply dishes a person a very full plate and you cope as best you can, trying to keep in mind that the problems you have at the moment are temporary. "Boundaries," usually necessary for good self-care, are temporarily suspended when people dear to me are vulnerable and hurting. Sometimes life is just plain difficult; I do what I can with it, realizing that someday I too will be vulnerable, and hoping that others will be kind to me when that day arrives. Yet I understood her point. All my socialization was against self-care, which, in my childhood home, was simply called "selfishness."

> What I do unto the least of my brethren, that I do unto Christ. But what if I should discover that the least among them all, the poorest of all the beggars, the most impudent of all the offenders, the very enemy himself—that these are all within me—that I myself stand in need of the alms of my own kindness—that I myself am the enemy who must be loved?
>
> —CARL JUNG

May 14, 2013

When his cell phone was not lost, as it often was, Owen called me very frequently. Because he confused night and day, he was often up at night, roaming the halls and calling me. I tried to teach him to look out the window to see if there is light or darkness, but he didn't understand, or couldn't remember. In desperation I turned off my cell phone at night, but sometimes he also called me on the land line. One night he called our dentist at 4 a.m. to ask him how the weather was. At that point I surreptitiously confiscated his address book.

Last night between the hours of 10:00 p.m. and 6:00 a.m. Owen called me twenty times—maybe more, because my voice mail was full and stopped recording calls.

Owen moved within the Berkshire several times. He first entered the independent living unit; then he moved to assisted living; he was in the hospital for a week after a fall and brain hematoma; then went to a rehab center for a couple of weeks, after which he returned, this time to the locked Recollections unit. When Owen first moved to the Recollections unit, one of the administrators took me on a tour. The residents were sitting around, most of them bent over, dozing. I cried, thinking of Owen living in this space with these people. A caregiver walked by and my tour guide started to introduce me, then she noticed that I was crying. So instead she said to the caregiver, "She's having a moment."

I noticed that after his falls, Owen was less aware and responsive than usual, more forgetful, and desperate to come home. After he settled down from the latest fall, everyone who observed Owen agreed that he did not belong in the dementia unit. So he moved again to the Assisted Living unit. However, several months later, after more falls he moved for the last time to the Recollections unit.

May 18, 2013

Today, on my seventy-sixth birthday, I had mixed emotions. I was profoundly grateful for my long life, which was richly rewarded professionally, but also included a great deal of personal pain. For many years I have articulated to myself—spelled out—that I am primarily working to transfer what Augustine called my psychic "weight" from fear to love.[3] *Fear, not hate, is the opposite of love. On many days it seems that I haven't gotten very far. I*

3. *Confessions* 13.9: "My weight is my love; by it I am carried wherever I am carried."

fear the future "bright with unshed tears," as that great philosopher, Pogo, said.

Owen called me, happy that he had remembered my birthday. "Happy birthday," he said, "now you are 84!" "No, I am 76," I told him, but at the end of a short conversation, he concluded, "Now you're 86!"

Owen called me on four different occasions to report that no meals had been served at The Berkshire for several days. The first few times he did this I became worried and inquired of caregivers if this was so; they reported that there had been meals as usual and that Owen had eaten them. He also frequently called me to complain that the staff wanted him to take a shower and change his clothes. One night he even called to thank me for placing him in such a wonderful residence where he has been "very happy for a number of years." Since he usually says that he "must get out of here," I found this quite amazing. Perhaps a new medicine was beginning to have an effect.

October 8, 2013

Owen is restless, calling during the night to say that he wants to come home, wants to live with me. I tell him that we will talk about it with his neurologist during his appointment next week. During the appointment I realized that doctors and caregivers are largely making educated guesses about what will help a dementia patient, trying this, trying that. Since each patient is different, and remedies affect different patients differently, it is difficult for doctors to know what to suggest. I told Owen's neurologist that it would help me a great deal if he would tell Owen that it's not possible for him to live at home. So he did the best he could. He said, in his quiet and rapid speech, "Your wife doesn't have the resources to care for you at home." Owen couldn't hear a word. The doctor also counseled Owen to "pick your battles," that is, not to protest taking a shower or putting on clean clothing. Owen did hear this and on the way home he kept repeating what good advice this was, and that he would remember it. The "good advice" did not, however, affect his behavior.

A well-intentioned friend wrote to say that people with dementia need routine and do best when they have it. When family members come to visit, she said, patients have many feelings they can't handle, from affection to irritation. "At some point it becomes clear that the facility staff (if they are kind) and the set routines of a place are more soothing to patients than relatives who come in and out and stir senses of obligation, affection, and confusion that must feel rather dislocating for all." She suggested that I gently back out of Owen's life, attending instead to my own life. This would be better for both of us, she advised.

Owen regularly tells me that he misses me, but I also miss him. Examining my motivation, I realize that I come to see him not only because I miss him, but also because, when he is gone, I don't want to be regretful or feel guilty that I did not do all I could for him. So I do not spend time with him only for his benefit. I examine the several layers of these complex feelings: Do I do things with and for Owen because I enjoy feeling virtuous? Because I want to keep him oriented to my visits, enjoying his claim that by coming to see him, as he frequently says, "I make a bad day into a good day"? Probably all of the above, but beyond all the complexity is the simple truth that I love him and miss him. Sometimes, as the French philosopher Michel Foucault said, "A pipe is only a pipe." And sometimes love should not be analyzed.

I am critical of the drift of psychotherapeutic language into popular speech. Terms such as "co-dependent" and "inappropriate" have no intrinsic meaning outside the particular perspective of the person using these words. They preclude real understanding and invite untrained people to "diagnose" others' intentions and behavior. Appropriating this dangerous "little knowledge" we, whose own behavior is often opaque to us, do not hesitate to label others' motivations and behavior!

Ever since Owen went to The Berkshire there have been multiple fraud attempts on his accounts. Blocking these frauds has required attentiveness and a great deal of paperwork. The first year I managed our income taxes, 2013, the IRS rejected my return because a woman I had never heard of had already filed a return as Owen's wife, using his name and social security number. Before my return was accepted I was required to supply many photocopied documents—from our wedding license to my Durable Power of Attorney for Finance—to establish that I was indeed Owen's wife. Perhaps the strangest scam was a letter summoning Owen to a criminal hearing two weeks hence at a county courthouse in Kentucky for a seven thousand dollar check he allegedly wrote three months after his death. That one was easy; I simply sent a copy of his death certificate.

Family finances were new to me; this was a part of our life that Owen had always managed. House maintenance was another steep learning curve for me. The foundation of our home on a Berkeley hill needed to be reinforced and the exterior painted. Appliances seemed to stop working as soon as Owen was not available to call service people—oven, furnace, garage door, vacuum cleaner. There was a gas leak and the roof leaked. I recognized how much Owen had done around the house and yard. I also took Owen to his several doctors, his dentist, and to hearing aid and optometrist appointments. The Berkshire staff would have taken him, but if I were not there, Owen would not have been able to articulate what was bothering him, and he could not have told me what the doctor said. Sometimes I was so overwhelmed with the many new things to do that I couldn't do anything and just sat frozen, catatonic.

Yesterday I picked up clothes that had been cleaned, took them to Owen, cleaned wax from his ears, cut and filed his nails, scheduled a haircut and beard trim for him, and checked on when the podiatrist is coming to cut his toenails. When he was at home, I cut his hair, weather permitting, on the deck. One day a strong wind knocked a bird's nest onto the deck from trees above us on the hill. Owen's silver hairs were woven through the twigs.

June 22, 2013

Today Owen called to tell me that The Berkshire residents had been served no meals for two days. Owen's anxiety about food puzzles me; he is acting like someone who has starved at some earlier time in his life, but this is not the case. It must be a dementia thing.

I'm sad that our life together has come to this. Both of us are hurting, yet there is still a great deal of tenderness. I rub lotion into his dry hands every day, caressing his hands a long time. Or I rub his shoulders. Sometimes he remarks that it feels good. I spend several hours with him every day, and almost always the overriding feeling I have is love for him. I am grateful that I don't often feel resentment that my life is so appropriated by Owen's illness.

November 5, 2014

Today it is raining. We need the rain badly, but I do not know if Ric is under a roof.

Chapter 6

INTERLUDE: CONNECTING THE PERSONAL AND THE SOCIAL

In chapter 2 I proposed a framework for situating discussion of the character of human nature. I considered three suggestions. First, Thucydides' *Melian Dialogue* proposed that that it is simply in the nature of things that "the strong take what they will, and the weak suffer what they must." Second, *The Epic of Gilgamesh* described a learning experience in which the hero came to realize that his desires must be negotiated in relation to others' desires and boundaries. In the Gilgamesh epic, the hero's untamed aggressiveness is effectively addressed by experience and education. Third, the Christian doctrine of original sin states that a component of nothingness or evil, mysteriously inherited from the first human beings, is an inevitable and permanent component of every human being. Struggle and education to overcome this dark spot do not work.

This chapter will suggest that in historically Christian societies the original sin theory retains a strong, unrecognized—strong *because* unrecognized—influence on personal and collective attitudes. Consider first the effect of the doctrine on a particular life. As a child in the home of a fundamentalist preacher, I was taught that like all children, I was "wicked from my mother's womb."[1] "I

1. Ps 51:6.

yearned to be a good girl, but I often found that I was a bad girl in others' eyes . . . It didn't take much to be considered bad in a fundamentalist household and community, and there was no distinction between 'bad acts' and a 'bad person.'"[2]

My parents learned the appropriate attitude to take toward their children from the trickle-down pronouncements of Christian authors like Martin Luther:

> Use the knife of God's Word to cut off the branches of [children's] contumacious will. Raise them in the fear of God. And when their wild nature comes up again—as weeds always will—and the old Adam sins in them again, kill it and bury it deep in the ground, lest the newly grown good nature once again revert to its wild state.[3]

Caspar Aquila, Lutheran Superintendent of Saxony in 1538, wrote a children's catechism that was intended to be learned and recited from an early age:

> Question: What have you learned from the Ten Commandments?
>
> Answer: I have learned the knowledge of our damnable sinful life.
>
> For the Ten Commandments are a book of vices to us in which we read clearly what we are before God without Grace, namely: idol worshippers, miscreants, blasphemers and despisers of God's divine name, cursed robbers of his holy temple, and renegades to his eternal word. We are disobedient abusers of our fathers, we are child murderers and envious dogs, killers, whoremongers, adulterers, thieves and rogues, dissemblers, liars, perjuring tale bearers, false witnesses, insolent misers. In sum, we are wild, insatiable beasts, against whose evil nature God erects the commandments as if they were high walls and locked gates.[4]

2. Miles, *Fundamentalist's Daughter*, 46.
3. Quoted by Strauss, *Luther's House*, 291.
4. Quoted in ibid.

I was not expected to memorize such catechisms, but my parents absorbed the attitudes enshrined in them through secondary sources—sermons, devotional literature, and several scriptural passages. Discussing these sixteenth-century childrearing manuals in my book *Augustine and the Fundamentalist's Daughter*, I concluded, "The message that I, when I am 'me,' am a sinner—that it is sin that defines me, my *self*—has been nearly impossible to eradicate."[5] The aftershock of my upbringing appears not only in my self-regard, but in the readiness with which the "original sin theory" presents itself as an appropriate understanding of others' motivation and behavior. Both personally and as a society, Americans are convinced that "the true self is aggressive, rude, dirty, disorderly, sexual; the false self, which mothers and society instruct us to assume, is neat, clean, tidy, polite, content to cut a chaste rosebud with silver-plated scissors."[6]

My personal example may not be shared by many people, but the "silent thought" that humans are inevitably undermined by original sin has bled into the assumptions of societies influenced by Christianity. While few Americans consciously agree with the original sin theory in the strong version quoted above, the social damages remain.

How is this evident in American society? I suggest that the social health of the nation, as researched at the Institute for Innovation in Social Policy at Vassar College, reflects rather dramatically the assumption that "losers" in our wealthy society deserve their suffering. The original sin theory is the umbilical cord that connects personal and social experience. Although this theory could be (and has been) interpreted as levelling the playing field (*every* human being participates in original sin), we do not assign its effects equally. We (as a society), cluster these effects in underprivileged and marginalized persons and groups, implying that those with privilege have overcome the undertow of original sin.

The Institute for Innovation in Social Policy, founded in 1986 at Fordham University, originally under the leadership of Marc and Marque-Luisa Miringoff, identified sixteen social indicators

5. Miles, *Fundamentalist's Daughter*, 21.

6. Malcolm, "Silent Woman."

that together measure the social health of the nation. The Institute regularly monitors these factors and has published reports in 2001, 2003, and 2008.[7] The indicators of social health used by the Institute are the following:

> Children: Infant mortality, child poverty, child abuse
>
> Youth: Teenage suicide, teenage drug abuse, high school completion
>
> Adults: Unemployment, average wages, health insurance coverage
>
> Aging: Poverty among the elderly, suicide among the elderly
>
> All ages: Homicides, alcohol-related traffic fatalities, food stamp coverage, affordable housing, income inequality.[8]

According to the above indicators, the Unites States is not a healthy nation. Twenty states are ranked as performing at below average levels. Populous states such as New York, California, Texas, and Florida are in this category. Ten additional states rank as average. Even the ten states ranked as excellent have only an average performance of 64.9. Minnesota, the top-ranked state, has a score of 75.0, while the lowest-ranked state, New Mexico, has a score of 26.8. The reports identify large discrepancies between states, indicating what—and *where*—specific improvements are most needed, providing information that can help activists and social agencies to target their attentions and labor.

The Institute's 2008 book focuses on social indicators' revelation of disparities between the states; their 1999 book compares American social health with that of other industrialized countries. *The Social Health of the Nation: How America Is Really Doing* sought to remedy the lack of regular reports on the nation's social health. Although the nation's finances are monitored and reported daily, reports on the nation's social health are incomplete and episodic. These two dimensions of national health—the economic

7. Opdycke and Miringoff, *The Social Health of the States, 2008*.

8. Ibid., 15.

and the social—are interrelated, but the effect of economic health on social health is not usually considered. The Institute's reports show that Americans are far more attentive to economic than to social health.

If social data were regularly reported, Americans would recognize that several key social indicators have worsened significantly over time and are currently performing at levels far below what was achieved in previous decades.

> Suicide rates among the young are 36% higher than they were in 1970 . . . Income inequality is at its third worst level in 50 years. More than 41 million Americans are without health insurance, the worst performance since records have been kept. Violent crime is almost double what it was in 1970 . . . Average wages for American workers have fallen sharply since the early 1970s . . . Approximately one in every five children in America today lives in poverty, a 33% increase since 1970.[9]

When American social health is compared with that of other industrialized nations, it is evident that Americans lag behind other societies. For example, twenty industrialized nations have fewer infant deaths (per 1000 live births) than the United States.[10]

Michael Moore's 2015 documentary film *Where to Invade Next* describes the significant progress being made by other industrialized nations in social indicators. In the film Moore interviews school administrators and dieticians, elected officials, prison wardens, and female and male workers in several European countries. Comparing many social indicators—from school lunches, to prison conditions, to paid vacations for workers—he discovered vast discrepancies between the experience and expectations of American citizens and those of citizens of some other nations.

Yet he also discovered that many of his interviewees cited the American dream as informing and influencing their idea of the common good. They take seriously, and translate into laws and

9. Miringoff and Miringoff, *Social Health*, 5.

10. Moreover, the rate of infant mortality is more than twice as high among African Americans as the white races, "a proportional gap that is higher than the one in 1970."

institutional policy, the American Constitution's statement that "life, liberty, and the pursuit of happiness" is the *right* of every human being. "Society just *works better*," Moore's interlocutors said, when children have time to play, when workers get generous paid vacation time, when convicts are given significant amounts of privacy and autonomy, and when citizens support the common good of the society rather than act out "each man for himself." In short, Moore found that "the American dream" is alive and active in many societies—just not in the United States.

I suggest that the "original sin theory" has infiltrated public assumptions in the United States, generating a fear culture in which human beings seek their own health, private wealth, and personal happiness, ignoring everyone else. Our fear generates greed for the *more* by which we attempt to fortify our material and emotional "belongings" against others' imagined eagerness to appropriate them at our direct expense. Self-aggrandizement results from the fear that someone else will get what is *owed me*. In the film, Michael Moore, playing devil's advocate, told a factory owner that he could earn a good deal more money if he did not give his employees so many paid vacations. The factory owner responded, "I don't need more money." Puzzled as to why he would want to limit his workers' paid leave, he added, "Then my employees would not be happy."

Our fears provoke the assumption that "bad behavior" indicates a "bad person." On the social level, fear is evident in the conflation of poor social indicators with the "bad people" who are forced to live in these conditions. It is assumed that bad people create bad social conditions; rather, poor conditions create desperate people, people who have learned from experience that alleviation of their living conditions will not come as a result of others' understanding and generosity, but must aggressively, often illegally, be seized.

Americans live in a culture of fear, a public culture in which fear factors, from diseases to wars, to killer bees, are regularly invoked by media.[11] Since fear factors fatigue in the public imagina-

11. Glassner, *Culture of Fear*, xvii.

tion, new factors are regularly identified to freshen our fear. And fears are often exaggerated. For example, Barry Glassner reports that in 2001, terrorist attacks killed 3,547 people *worldwide*, while 42,000 Americans were killed in motor vehicle accidents.[12] Terrorism has become a major source of public fear, while motor vehicle deaths are not featured in the news unless famous people are involved. My point is not that there is no reason to fear; human beings with our vulnerable bodies always have reason to fear disease and accident. But the *culture of fear* in which we live actively contributes to taking "our attention and energies away from creatively addressing the pressing problems of American society, encouraging attitudes of passivity and helplessness."[13]

The cynicism and passivity that fuel our culture of fear are strong enemies. Yet horrifying stories and images that claim to "raise consciousness," actually reinforce our fear rather than urging us to action. Shock tactics are not working. Would love, which is reputed to carry a force powerful enough to "cast out fear," stimulate positive change? If so, how can the force of love be summoned and directed, for it is equally true that fear has the ability to cast out love? Media versions of romantic love have stifled a broader sense of love that will be needed to inspire efforts on behalf of the *common* good—love of life and love of the "fellow pilgrims" with whom we share this beautiful world, love that is powered by gratitude and responsibility. Rather than the passive condition we know as "falling in love," we can recover the *activity* of *making* love. Love cannot be commanded but it can be *made*.

> Love has feet . . . Love has hands which give to the poor, love has eyes which give information about who is in need, love has ears . . . To see love's activity is to see God.
>
> —AUGUSTINE

12. Since Glassner wrote in 2001, the events of 9/11 in New York City have supported and escalated Americans' fear of terrorism.

13. Braver, *Friends*, 181.

As Michael Moore advocated, we could learn from the example of other nations who are effectively changing conditions that had appeared to be intractable. We can observe, and learn with humility—not an attitude that Americans are known for in the rest of the world—commitments and methods by which other industrialized societies are creating change for the *common* good. Jettisoning our silent belief in the dark, infantilizing, and destructive undertow of original sin, we can work with the active energy of love. Placing our faith in the human *tabula rasa*, we can learn how to call forth, sustain, and build on the active and intentional love that makes individual lives and the lives of societies productive, pleasurable, and happy.

Chapter 7

MOST BEAUTIFUL WOMAN IN THE WORLD

> He ain't give you nothing you can't bear, Rose. But had He? Maybe this one time He had. Had misjudged and misunderstood her particular backbone. This one time. This here particular spine.
>
> —Toni Morrison

Owen's doctor recommended that he reenter the "Recollections" maximal care unit at The Berkshire. When a shared room became available in June 2014, Owen moved. The rooms in that unit opened onto a main hall so that caregivers could keep an eye on what was happening in the rooms as they walked along the hall—not quite a panopticon, but close. The unit is locked, requiring a combination to exit.

The atmosphere in Recollections was markedly different from that of the assisted living section. Sharing a room with another dementia patient required mutual patience. When Owen or I entered his room, his first roommate bellowed, "Get out of here and stay out." Owen said to me, "Just ignore him." Every couple of minutes a patient down the hall called for his Mama to come and help him, a plaintive cry to which the staff and residents, having heard it so continuously, seemed oblivious. Three muttering and/or humming women residents—I called them the "Three Graces"—strolled the unit together, picking up and examining objects in various rooms before putting them down or carrying them away and setting them down randomly in other rooms. In the dining room some of the residents slouched over their food, eating nothing until a caregiver fed them; some were fed by private caregivers hired by families. Still others like Owen fed themselves but without apparent enjoyment, spilling food on themselves or the floor with every bite. The food was good, but uninspiring. No one conversed with someone else, though several carried on monologues with themselves. One man occasionally and unpredictably screamed, and was taken to eat by himself in the hall outside.

There was a pleasant enclosed garden to which residents had free access, and Owen and I frequently sat outside when the weather was good. We admired four very tall palm trees on the street outside the garden, and we watched birds or the bees working the flowers. Owen had a particular fondness for the large crows that flew by. He sometimes mimicked their "language" as they cawed. Once he remarked to his son, "I *need birds!*" From time to time a determined resident tried unsuccessfully to climb over the fence into the parking lot beyond.

The day after Owen entered the Recollections unit, he was not in his room when I visited, and I couldn't find him. I looked, the staff looked; since the unit is locked, he had to be *somewhere.* Finally I walked down the hall, looking in all the rooms, and found him sleeping in someone else's room, in someone else's bed. He looked very small and fragile, sleeping there in strange surroundings.

Overworked caregivers take residents to the shower when they have a few minutes to spare, scrubbing them hastily and vigorously. Owen hated showers. Showers, he told me, were "painful and embarrassing" and "take three hours." He insisted that he would take a shower when *he* wanted to take a shower, not when a caregiver wanted him to. One day he confided in me that the *only* reason caregivers wanted him to have a shower was so that they could see him naked. He was serious; I was amused at the thought of these mostly middle-aged, brown-skinned women caregivers longing to see a skinny ninety-year-old naked white man.

Clothing "circulated" in the Recollections unit. In spite of writing Owen's name on his clothes, I frequently saw other old men in his shirts, sweaters, and jackets. I also often saw Owen in others' shirts, pants, shoes, and slippers. So-called permanent ink, I discovered, is often unreadable after repeated washings. The random collection of clothes hanging in Owen's closet contributed to some peculiar "fashion statements." After a few frustrating and unsuccessful efforts to recover Owen's clothes, I decided that this issue came squarely under the category of *unimportant.* But when Owen's gold retirement watch disappeared I alerted caregivers who blithely told me, "It will turn up." And indeed it did! A caregiver noticed it walking around on the wrist of another old man. Under the pretext of admiring it, she examined it and found Owen's name engraved on the back. Residents could never be accused of stealing; they did not have the ability to premeditate or steal with intent. Therefore, an adjusted vocabulary was necessary for describing these exchanges. Something "goes missing"; then, unless it—like a hearing aid battery—is small enough to be sucked up by the vacuum cleaner, it almost invariably "turns up."

There were few friendships among residents in the Recollections unit. Each of the patients was occupied by the private movie playing in her/his own mind. Often they sat in a cluster with others, but they were apparently uninterested in communicating, or perhaps unable. Some were very talkative, but their talk was repetitious and limited to their mental tape.

On the other hand, family members who visited frequently often formed strong friendships with one another. Friends are important as never before, for there is no loneliness like the loneliness of being with a loved who is not with you. Each of us knew what the others were experiencing because we were experiencing it too. We exchanged sympathy, support, advice, gossip, and whenever possible, laughter. Sometimes these friendships survived the immediate situation, emerging intact into the so-called real world beyond the Berkshire.

October 31, 2014

When I came to see Owen today he was sleeping and could not be roused. His breathing was labored and I thought he had a throat rattle. I was convinced that he was dying. I called his son, saying that I thought he might be dying. Addie came, and he told me that his mother, Owen's first wife, had died in Seattle several hours before. Owen didn't wake. I cried off and on for the six hours I sat with him. Finally the caregiver who had been on duty the night before, came and talked with me. She said that she didn't think he was dying; he was sleeping so strongly, she said, because he'd been "up all night." She bent over him to listen to his "rattle," then stood up and said, "Margaret, that's snoring." I went home and called Owen's son to apologize for alarming him on the day his mother died which, of course, I hadn't known when I called. He was very kind and said that I had done the right thing to call when I thought that Owen was dying.

The peripheral role of religion among dementia patients surprised and puzzled me. One Sunday morning when I came to the unit to dress Owen in clean clothes before taking him to church, the residents were gathered in the common room singing. They sang Christian hymns interspersed with popular songs of an earlier time—like "Bicycle built for two," and "I could have danced all night." In their quavering voices they sang the children's hymn, "Jesus loves me, this I know." I knew that several of the singers were Jewish, and I guessed that several others were atheists. "Are all the patients Christian?" I said, as innocently as possible, to the caregiver-in-charge. She got my drift—something about the exclusion of non-Christians—and she fixed me with a steely eye and said, "They're *just* singing." I didn't press my point.

Owen calls and calls, "What am I supposed to do here?" I try to advise him. I tell him that he could provide a very valuable service where he is. He has been a priest, ordained in the Episcopal Church, for more than sixty years. People around him are lonely and frightened; he could befriend them, sit with them, listen to them. Just be with. He need not give advice in order to be helpful; anyway he is not the "come to Jesus" kind of priest. This possibility for "ministry" did not appeal to him. He insisted that he must earn money in order to take care of people who depend on him. He is, quite literally, deaf to my reassurance that he *has* taken care of the people who need his care and now it was his turn to be cared for. He has not outlived his male socialization to provide financially for family, still feeling that responsibility strongly.

The skills I most appreciated from Owen—money and house management—are tasks that now require of me a very steep learning curve. But I am also very grateful that he uncomplainingly took care of this range of tasks for many years so that I could write books! This was indeed a great luxury. I may wish that I had paid more attention to tasks that now baffle me and, especially in my present "grief-mind," are difficult to learn. I read that "grief-mind" is very similar to dementia; sometimes (briefly) I must stop and think what day it is, and sometimes I forget appointments! Now perhaps I know something of the frustration Owen must have felt as memory and abilities deserted him!

> Send me forth into another life
> lord because this one is growing faint
> I do not think it goes all the way.
>
> —W. S. Merwin

Atul Gawande's book *Being Mortal* criticizes assisted-living residences' preoccupation with safety, a value that effectively precludes attention to residents' well-being, autonomy, privacy, and interest in life. Certainly, it was these quality-of-life issues that Owen obsessed on in the Recollections unit. Gawande does not explore differences between men's and women's differing values, but even in advanced dementia, these are quite significant. Privacy and autonomy seem to be more important to men than to women, who are likely to be more accustomed to negotiating their needs with those of others. Owen's complaint that the staff only wanted him to take a shower so they could see him naked protested a lack of privacy. His attempt to insist that he would take a shower "when I want to take a shower," rather than when "they want me to," protested a lack of autonomy. The staff was kind, albeit tired and overworked, unable to accommodate privacy and autonomy. Indeed, as Owen complained, the "virtues" appreciated by administrators and caregivers were those associated with children: obedience, alacrity, and acceptance of authority in the most fundamental decisions of daily life—what to wear, when to brush teeth, and when to shower.

However, in spite of arranging caregivers' work for maximal efficiency, even safety measures were often ineffective. For example, Owen could not be prevented from falling; a caregiver would need to be at his side every minute, night and day, to modify what a nurse euphemistically called his "independence." Toward the end of his life he fell almost every day. He died with cuts and bruises on his head and body from these falls. I often cried when I greeted him and saw new wounds from falls. He could not be persuaded to move more slowly and *always* with his walker and helmet. The falls were directly related to his insistence on exercising whatever autonomy he could. Clearly, for Owen, privacy and autonomy were integral to an existence that felt like life.

Gawande's suggestions for bringing *life* into a residence are labor-intensive—pets, dogs, cats, and birds roaming freely, children interacting with the residents—all these life-giving innovations require more energy than a tired, overworked staff can manage. Can institutions with financial limitations (at least partially caused by the maintenance of a profit margin acceptable to administrators), provide more than kindness, a measure of safety, and personal care?

Although it is often impossible for families to keep loved ones in their homes, families are still important. Most of the families I observed did their best to take their loved ones on small excursions—perhaps even a walk around the block—and to bring favorite foods, music, or books. One resident's creative and generous wife bought her husband a small electric scooter and took him to a park to ride it, an expensive effort to give her husband pleasure. He enjoyed it greatly on two or three outings but was very soon incapable of the necessary balance. Even with the best of intentions, not all families have the necessary time, money, and energy to bring resources to residents.

In short, Gawande's suggestions for the future of assisted-living residences require (1) different architecture (single rooms), and (2) flexible staff (willing, for example, to clean up animal messes), and time to listen and respond to residents' desires and longings. These are not changes that can occur overnight. As long-term visions they are undoubtedly wonderful. But in the meantime, despite programs of group exercises and outings for assisted-living residents, in the Recollections unit it is largely left to family members to bring freshness and pleasure—life—to their loved ones. On the other hand, people are different from one another even in old age and dementia. A case can also be made for families' benign neglect of residents. One set of instructions—emphatically does not fit all.

April 2, 2014

Owen called to tell me that I am "the most beautiful woman in the world." "When are you coming to see me?" "Where shall I meet you?" he asked repeatedly. "Don't worry," I told him, "I will find you."

May 2, 2014

Last evening I had a remarkable phone call from Owen. He thanked me for placing him in such a "wonderful residence," where he has been "very happy for a number of years." This was amazing to me; he usually insists that he "must get out of here."

But between that evening and the next morning, I heard quite a different story: he complained that the staff was stealing his clothes and selling them!

July 5, 2014

On the Fourth of July, the Recollections unit had a lunch to which family members were invited. It was a beautiful day so most of us were sitting outside in the garden. An African American resident's family was there—several happy and gregarious middle-aged women and a teenaged boy—daughters and a grandson, I speculated. When the party was over, they went home. After a few minutes I happened to look over at the old man; he was perfectly still and making no sound, but tears were running down his face. Just as I noticed this, a caregiver also noticed. She sat down next to him and held his hand. She said nothing; there was nothing to say. Instead she gave her presence.

By a strange coincidence, Owen's tennis partner when we were on sabbatical in Rome in 1983 was also in Recollections. Bill, mostly catatonic, without speech, and unable to feed himself, was being pushed in a wheelchair by a caregiver down the hall where Owen and I were sitting. I smiled and greeted him. Glancing over at us, Bill said one word, "Nice."

One day, sitting by Owen's bed, I heard an old African American man walking down the hall singing quietly to himself, "I'm coming, I'm coming, for my head is bending low. I hear those gentle voices calling old black Joe."

November 28, 2014

In the Canadian film Jesus of Montreal someone asks a young woman why she sleeps with the old priest. She replies, "Because it gives him so much pleasure and me so little pain." I recognize that this rationale underlies many of the things I do. In my mind I maximize the pleasure that Owen will get from what I do, and minimize what it will cost me. Yesterday, Thanksgiving, is an example. I thought it would give Owen "so much pleasure" to go to Bolinas, to my daughter's home, for the day. I wanted to have Thanksgiving dinner with my family, so I thought it would give me "so little pain" to take him. He loved Bolinas, where we had lived for a year, 1994–95, when Owen had retired and I was on sabbatical. But the outing gave him less pleasure, and it gave me considerably more pain than I anticipated. He knew my daughter's home quite well, but he became disoriented. Dinner was later than planned, the turkey taking longer than expected to cook. This disturbed him; he wasn't hungry, he had been snacking on hors d'oeuvres all afternoon, but he became loudly anxious about driving home in the dark. Everyone was affected. Susan, my daughter, who had carefully timed when the turkey would be ready to serve, was upset that it wasn't ready. Another guest was trying to talk to Owen, but told me that he found it difficult because Owen seemed not to hear and did not respond. I tried to distract Owen. I had planned to take him for a walk, but realized that it was impossible to take him (with his walker), for a walk on the beach, or even on the surrounding rough country roads. Finally, dinner was ready, but because of Owen's continuing agitation and anxiety, we left before dessert. Driving home, Owen was panicked, saying repeatedly that he didn't know the way. I assured him that I knew the way and that I was driving very carefully. He was unconvinced. In short, compared to the work involved, Thanksgiving was not a day that gave either of us—or Susan's company—much pleasure. Owen was visibly relieved when I returned him to The Berkshire.

In March 2015, I asked the rector of the small Episcopal church we had been attending, when Owen was still able, to bring communion to him. Julie agreed and came to The Berkshire with her communion kit. Owen was sleeping when she arrived. I woke him and got him sitting on the bed. She spoke to him gently while spreading out the communion paraphernalia. As soon as she put out the wafers, he quickly grabbed and ate them. During the short readings and prayers he asked loud questions: "Where are you living now?" It saddened me greatly to see that he was unable to recognize a ritual he must have experienced thousands of times. (He taught at a seminary that had daily chapel with communion.) He didn't say the Lord's Prayer—and neither could I because of my tears. Julie, however, was unflappable. She carried on, shortening the service when she understood that he was not participating.

Why am I unable simply to accept that Owen is dying rather than grieve over every new evidence of the fact? And why doesn't a religious life, faithfully practiced for many years, help more *in extremis*? In the more than thirty-five years I had known him, Owen always read the daily office, the scripture readings of the liturgical year prescribed for priests. We also read a psalm together every morning before beginning our days. I was deeply shaken to see how little his religion seemed to help him. Does the solace of religious beliefs fade when understanding is lost?

Considering this question for many days and nights, I came to the conclusion that at some moment in the process of gradually or rapidly losing functions of body and mind—from loss of bowel and bladder control to loss of memory—those who love the dying person must carry on religious practice on his/her behalf. Just as we help with dressing, eating, and physical necessities, just as we attempt to help them remember the events and people they loved. We cannot know what comforts and sustains our loved one. *Not knowing* if he remembers, recognizes, feels, or understands the words and rituals we have shared, we can, with the confidence of our years of life and practice together, repeat the words and perform the rituals; we simply offer what we have. Years ago Owen told me of a dying friend and colleague of his who drew his last breath at the moment the ritual of last rites (*viaticum*) ended. Indeed, Owen's own death occurred as a priest friend prayed at his bedside. But we are not quite there yet.

I searched for activities that Owen could enjoy, fresh air he could breathe. The search was limited by his poor hearing. His expensive hearing aids, lost and replaced several times, didn't seem to help, so he couldn't enjoy listening to music or being read to. Ordinary conversation had to be shouted if he was to hear, so we didn't converse much. He enjoyed going to the "bistro" in the assisted living unit where snacks were provided—coffee, tea, juices, yogurt, fruit, cookies, and cereal. We often sat in another lovely garden at the Berkshire while he drank coffee and ate cookies. He was unable to hear the mourning doves that flew from one balcony to another, but I heard them, cooing gently. Sometimes we went to the small library on the second floor and looked at old *National Geographic* magazines, with pictures of beautiful scenery, strange animals, or people with decorated faces and bodies.

> But still for us existence is enchanted: from a
> hundred places
> it is still origin. A play of pure forces
> that no one touches unless he kneels and admires.
>
> —Rilke

For about two years, Owen's favorite outing was a short car trip to the Berkeley Marina. On the way he remarked many times what a beautiful day it was and pointed out the crows cawing and cavorting. He also read aloud the many signs on University Avenue, always commenting that San Pablo Avenue was named for St. Paul. As we neared the marina his excitement grew. "Here comes the bread car," he announced to the seagulls, eager to throw to them the bread crumbs I had brought. His delight in seeing the birds squawking and fighting over the crumbs continued until a few months before his death, when he seemed to suddenly tire of it. Sometimes we walked (with his walker) along the long bumpy

Berkeley pier to see the sailboats, the Golden Gate Bridge, and what—if anything—the fishermen were catching.

> And the true joy of the long dead child sang burning in the sun.
>
> —Dylan Thomas

I too enjoyed these outings. In fact I sought activities that I also enjoyed so that I would not begin to feel resentful that so much of my life was devoted to Owen. I also enjoyed sitting outside in the gardens at the Berkshire and taking him to parks for short walks. This was an important consideration since, at the time, it seemed that the long goodbye would go on forever, each day quite similar to the last—and the next.

February 1, 2015

I was invited to provide an article on a subject of my choice for a new Encyclopedia of Religion. Attracted as I was to the invitation—when is an academic invited to write on a subject of her choice?—I nevertheless knew that I must decline. The circumstances of my life did not allow me to concentrate on a scholarly article. I grieved over this decision, fearing that if I continue to decline scholarly invitations I will no longer be invited.

> You're not really awake when you don't write. And you have no idea who you are. Not to mention who you aren't.
>
> —Pascal Mercier

February 17, 2015

More falls. This morning I found Owen with a battered forehead and top of his head. The nurse with whom I discussed Owen's condition said that a wheelchair would not help because Owen is so "independent"—I think she meant "stubborn"—that he would frequently get out of the chair, giving more opportunities for falls. He was muttering to himself, making no sense. He seemed to be in pain, saying that it hurt to sit and that his bowels hurt. He was often constipated, perhaps caused by the medicines prescribed for dementia patients.

His caregiver suggested that he should be signed up for hospice. Hospice nurses, she said, can provide another level of monitoring and recommendations for care. So I asked his physician for a written statement that, in his best judgment, Owen will die within six months—the criterion for hospice care. While the nurse and I talked, Owen repeated the same nonsense words again and again. Oh my poor Owen. I loved him when he was here to love, and I love him still, but now as my helpless child.

February 19, 2015

Clearly I was right to decline the writing project. Over the weekend The Berkshire called three times to tell me that Owen is acting strangely. He doesn't speak intelligibly, just mumbles. And he has more cuts on his head.

He entered hospice care in March 2015. With hospice, *we don't need to know whether he has a disease or how to cure it, we just need to minimize the pain.* Grief takes me unpredictably; I think, "Oh my poor little Owen"—and he *is* little, weighing 106 pounds and losing steadily. I feel myself a channel for the love of everyone who has ever loved him, from his parents forward, his daily conduit of love. I want him to sail out into the universal life on love.

Look, we don't love like flowers, with only a single
season behind us; immemorial sap
mounts in our arms when we love.

—Rilke

This is what I want for myself when my time comes: to have a vivid feeling of the richness, love, and beauty of life. In short, to move "out of death, into the larger life." But not as the individual "me." Plotinus, said that life, by definition, cannot die. "It is simply no longer *there*" (in my exhausted body).[1] When we die, he said, our individual life joins the great circulation of life in the universe.

March 25, 2015

A very frustrating day at the Berkshire: Owen in pain, constipated, then losing bowel control, a huge mess. Owen cried in frustration. On the way home I decided that I needed to pamper myself. I bought a dozen gorgeous roses—cream with orange outlining the tips of the petals, smelling beautiful. At home, I listened to a restful CD while drinking a glass of wine. I ordered shoes on the Internet and read a good novel.

Sometimes I feel sad about the many hours of my life I spend with Owen every day. Sometimes I only watch him sleep because he has been awake, prowling the hall the night before.

April 8, 2015

The other day Owen said, "Thanks for being gentle with me."

The hospice nurse said that she sees a rapid decline in Owen in the last week. She ordered oxygen in order to be prepared when he needs help to breathe.

Owen told a caregiver that his mother and his wife were coming to see him. There is a strange truth here. Giving him motherly care, loving him as a mother, I have become his mother to him; his mother and his wife are the same person. And I *was* coming to see him! Every day I rub his hands with lotion because they are dry and cold. Every week I bring manicure tools from home to clip and

1. Plotinus, *Ennead* 4.5.7.

file his nails; he is not allowed to have cutting tools in his room—if he does, they disappear.

Owen is bewildered. He asks questions that make no sense, wanting his reality confirmed. Replying to his questions I usually can only say thoughtfully, "I don't know." Sometimes I simply agree with whatever he says. Or I try to deflect his inner movie. I say, "Let's be *here* right now. Look at that beautiful tree with all the tiny raindrop diamonds on its branches."

> It is difficult enough to breathe in and out, remain vertical, and remember one's temporary address.
>
> —Kate Braverman

Once he told me that he had "walked the streets" (meaning the hall) all morning (meaning all night), looking for a job, and no one would give him one. He repeats that he needs to make money because people depend on him. I tell him again that he has taken care of his family all his life; now others will take care of him.

April 27, 2015

I took Owen to the Berkeley marina this morning, a beautiful warm morning. He was happy and commented frequently on the beauty of the day. When I brought him back to the Berkshire for lunch I sat by him as he ate hungrily. He asked me what he should do this afternoon. I said that he could take a nap, and then go outside to sit in the garden when he wakes up. "I don't think I'll wake up," he said off-handedly. When I took him to his room after lunch to settle him for his nap he kept hugging me and thanking me for "everything" I do for him. I kissed him, told him that I love him, and that I would see him tomorrow. I turned to look at him as I walked out and he waved. I went home crying, realizing that this could have been good bye. Indeed, it may have been the last time he was conscious enough to realize that he was leaving me.

May 1, 2015

I am not going to The Berkshire today. Yesterday, while Owen was asleep, his roommate urinated in the wastebasket, oblivious to my presence in the room. Suddenly I'd had enough of the Recollections unit; I left, saying to a caregiver, "I'm tired of old men!"

In spite of some incidents like this, I was fortunate in my experience with Owen. Several of the residents did not give any sign of recognizing family members; yet their wives, lovers, sons and daughters, showed up, day after day, week after week, month after month. I was well rewarded for my attention to Owen. In his last year, Owen became more affectionate than he had been in our thirty-four years of marriage. He proclaimed loudly, "I love you, Margaret," several times every day. He frequently commented that my arrival made "a bad day good," and he often said, "You are the most beautiful woman in the world."

His new, or newly expressed, affection was the great gift to me of his last year or so. At the age of ninety-two he was finally free to feel and to express feeling. Family members of other residents also told me stories of their loved ones, old men I forgivingly call "men of their generation," socialized to be stoical, aggressive, and unfeeling. Like Owen in his last months, some of them became sweet and capable of uncharacteristic generosity, even though they were not always free of feelings of suspicion and persecution.

May 18, 2015

Today Owen's hospice doctor ordered morphine for him. I hope it helps his pain, but it is also a sad acknowledgment that he is in the last days of his life.

I spent most of a long day clearing Owen's study of boxes and boxes of paper, from instruction manuals for appliances we have not owned for years, to old sermons and class lectures. I suspect that Owen had never thrown away a piece of paper with writing on it! I came upon a box in a corner of the topmost shelf that had a note scotch-taped to the top: Please destroy without opening. So I did. The box was in the house overnight, and I took it to be shredded the next morning, fearing that if it were at home any longer I might, in a weak moment, open it. I don't need to know Owen's secrets; they might distress me, and they would not change my love for him.

> June 3, 2015
>
> *More falls. Owen simply cannot slow down, move more deliberately and carefully, and consistently use his walker and padded helmet. A recent fall sent him to the Emergency Room with cuts on his face and neck; the neck cut needed stitches.*

Brian, the son of Owen's roommate, has a daily ritual with his father. Sitting with his father outside, weather permitting, he peels an orange, sections it, and they slowly eat it together. For several days, one of the other residents came and stood before them watching as they shared the orange. Brian asked him if he too would like an orange and Richard, who does not talk, nodded. So now Brian brings two oranges. He carefully peels and sections one of them for Richard.

In May 2015 I had a bad cold and cough for more than a month. Nothing I usually do to minimize a cold worked. I even went to bed for two days. How can I be more protective of my health? Owen repeats again and again that he is so glad to see me when I appear each day. It's impossible for me to see that my daily visits make him happy—and not continue to do it. My doctor diagnosed bronchitis and pneumonia and gave me a strong antibiotic that stopped the cough within two days.

I reread my old journals and see that I have been writing about his dementia since 2005—a full decade. I must try harder, relax more, and find the activities that strengthen me—and all at once! Meanwhile, "back at the ranch," I am dealing with fraud attempts on Owen's accounts, trying to decide what to do with the house, and beginning to plan for an inevitable memorial service.

I also grieve over Ric, but I know that I am giving him what I can give him, namely a case worker who does what he can for Ric. When my sister and her husband were here I showed them a picture of ten-year-old Ric and told them that at that age Ric was writing acceptance speeches for when he would be elected president of the United States. The contrast—then and now—is appalling. He was a beautiful little blond boy with delicate features and a great deal of energy. Now he is fifty-seven; his teeth are falling out and those that remain are brown. He is skinny with a pot belly from beer and malnutrition. These days I cry over "my men"—Owen and Ric—several times a day. I struggle to say "the right thing," the words that will get their attention and inspire change. But it doesn't matter what I say. Words will not make difference, either to Owen's safety or to Ric's sobriety. A "word person" like me finds it difficult to accept that words—the right words—are not magic. I keep trying.

June 6, 2015

Today is our 34th wedding anniversary. We've had happier anniversaries, but I will take Owen some chocolate and we'll celebrate. We'll eat it with coffee, sitting outside in the garden. The occasion has made me weepy, thinking about our marriage, its strengths and its disappointments. On the whole it has been a good marriage, but one in which both of us were somewhat lonely—perhaps that's nothing but the human condition: we are born and we die alone. In his last days, Owen tried to stay with me, but dementia patients can't always do that.

June 22, 2015

Owen's last trip to the emergency room after another fall occurred only a week before he died. The day before he fell he turned to me as I was sitting with him while he ate lunch and said, "What can I do to make your life easier?" I replied, "Don't fall. Move more slowly and carefully so you don't fall. Use your walker and wear your helmet." His concern for me was touching, his intentions were good, but his memory was poor. The next day he fell, causing multiple bruises and abrasions on his arms and legs and a bleeding cut under his left eye.

He was talking loudly but incoherently when I joined him in the Emergency Room, and he was trying to pull out the intravenous wires in his arms. I stayed as long as I could, holding his hands so he couldn't pull out the tubes. Owen's agitated, stubborn side is now exacerbated by dementia. After several hours I gave up tearfully and went home.

He was admitted to the hospital that evening, but was sent back to the Berkshire the next day. The Emergency Room doctor told me that sending him "home" with hospice was the best thing we could do for him. Not much; not enough—just send him back and wait for the next fall? It makes a cruel kind of sense that he will die, not with a whimper, but with a bang—a fall.

June 29, 2015

Today Owen is restless; he is unconscious and his agitation seems to indicate that he is in pain, even though he is on a heavy dose of morphine. I talked gently to him, reciting Psalm 23 several times. Close to his ear I sang softly "The King of Love My Shepherd Is," "Love Divine All Loves Excelling"—our wedding hymns—and "Amazing Grace." He seemed to quiet as I sang.

Life is not undone by death—nor a single moment by all the moments that come after it.

—Wayne Johnston

Owen died on June 29, 2015, about 8:15 in the evening. For several days he had been asleep or unconscious, on morphine. Because of his earlier inability to understand when communion was brought to him, I did not arrange the *viaticum*, or last rites, for him. But he had an impromptu version of last rites anyway. On the evening he died I was sitting with him, planning to spend the night. I had been at his bedside for many long hours when a priest friend called to offer to come and sit with me for an hour. I was happy to have her company. After we sat together awhile, I took the opportunity to leave Owen with her and went to the bathroom. While I was away for two or three minutes, Flora said a prayer aloud. She also told Owen that it was all right for him to go. When I returned she said, "He isn't breathing." I kissed him, stroked his face, and cried. As soon as I was able to talk I called his son who came within minutes. The hospice nurse was there and she made the necessary calls, returning to tell me that the mortuary would come for Owen within an hour. I left; I couldn't bear to see them take him away. My friend, concerned that I should not be driving, wanted to drive me home, but I assured her that I had driven home crying many times from the Berkshire and knew how to be extra careful. She followed me to make sure that I got home safely. We sat together for a while.

> When the body perishes, how would the life still remain?
> Well, then has this life perished? No, certainly not, for this
> too is the image of a radiance; it is simply no longer there.
>
> —Plotinus

Chapter 8

POSTLUDE

> Glad to have ridden the big waves,
> Glad to be very quiet now.
> —May Sarton

Dementia patients often appear to be intentionally subverting caregivers' efforts on their behalf. Their families are tempted to suspect that the "true self," characterized by original sin, is showing through the façade of civilized behavior. "What next?" I asked repeatedly, fearing the worst. It is easy to extrapolate fear of the loved one's dangerous behavior to a broader fear of assault from other family members, neighbors, and people encountered in public spaces. In this mood fear directs my expectations and my interpretation of others' motivations and behavior.

Sometimes, however, dementia patients are loving, appreciative of their care, and sweet. Which behavior should I consider the true self? Again, this is the wrong question. The true self is all of the above. A bottom line cannot be identified. Owen's son, Addie, took several pictures of him in his last days; in these pictures Owen's sweetness is very evident. "Sweetness" is not a word I use often, and would not have used of Owen in earlier days; I had thought of sweetness as synonymous with "saccharine," namely, artificial and forced. Now I understood its meaning. In his last months I enjoyed his sweetness, but I was also distracted by trying to figure out how to prevent another fall, how to get him to eat, whether his medicines were right, and especially whether he was free of pain. Now that his death has released me from worry about him, I see his sweetness very clearly. I arbitrarily choose to think that I am finally seeing Owen as "himself"; he had outlived his socialization to the twentieth-century American idea of maleness. Near the end of his life his earlier urgent sense that he needed to earn money to take care of people for whom he was responsible disappeared, as did any tendency to aggressiveness. He became gentle and loving.

A friend described her mother in a convalescent hospital at the end of her life. My friend was startled when caregivers told her that her mother was sweet; when she was growing up she had not experienced her mother as sweet. My friend interpreted her mother's dramatic change as the result of her calculation that if she was "nice" to her caregivers, they would be nice to her. I don't think so; the dementia patients I have known did not have the ability to calculate their behavior and its effects. The dying people I have been with in the Recollections unit and earlier as a hospice volunteer were shedding lifelong attitudes, actions, and reactions. They were relaxing from stressful ways of relating to other human beings and the world.

Dying, and the process of dying, is the final "getting over oneself." My mother, who often said that she refused to be happy until all of her four children were happy, on her deathbed suddenly said, "I'm happy." I think that she was feeling released from her perennial worry about her children, who were never all happy at once.

In his last months and weeks, Owen was peaceful. Yes, there were aspects of the Recollections unit that he did not like—showers, for example—but he never became angry. A friend was not so fortunate. Her husband, heavily medicated for pain, loudly blamed her for his predicament, a harsh return for her loving care. Even though she was told that his pain drugs were known to result in uncharacteristic behavior, she could not help wondering if his anger was based on hitherto repressed resentment. After he died it was difficult for her to forget those days at the end of his life.

In order to *be with* a loved one who is dying, one must also "get over oneself," letting go of old grievances. If the loved one is a parent, sibling, or spouse, one must let go of old memories of distressing words and actions, childhood presumptions of unfairness, and lingering suspicions that my parent loved a sibling more than s/he loved me. I must discard these carefully hoarded and highly selective memories. I must recognize that I have assiduously cultivated these particular memories (and not others) in order to explain and justify lifelong resentment. Just as the dying person gets over "himself" as life ebbs, so one who loves him also has some work to do in this *new* relationship. And we do not have infinite time to adjust old patterns of thought and behavior. The long goodbye may seem to go on forever, but it doesn't; tomorrow is never assured. Of course, no one is assured of tomorrow, but most of us have the luxury of ignoring that fact.

Recently I read an article that admonished readers to greet every day saying, "I can and I will." In fact, I have sometimes found it important to acknowledge that I can't and I won't! I can't and I won't cure my son of alcoholism, and I was unable to keep Owen from falling frequently. On occasions such as these, a more realistic acknowledgment is, I did the best I could and it wasn't enough—simultaneously a sad and a freeing admission—*just what there is.* Nobody can do more than their best with life's difficulties. But I must also acknowledge, rather than conceal from myself, that my efforts were not—*and could not have been*—enough to change my loved one's behavior.

After a loved one's death, it becomes important not to undermine one's readjustment to ordinary life by regret. Instead, I tried to remember more honestly the times there were. In the fatigue of the daily visits there were times when I desperately *needed* to take a day off. I may *wish* that I had been capable of infinite energy, but the truth that I must admit to myself is that I was not—am not. Yes, I did the best I could, and it is also true that my best *was not enough.* To acknowledge both simultaneously is to real-ize my humanity.

Similarly, I can never be sure that I have understood a circumstance thoroughly enough to be able truthfully to say about it, "I know." Very often I must acknowledge that "I don't know." Plato advised his friends to avoid the "double ignorance," namely, I don't know, and I don't know that I don't know. I am often tempted to *think* that I know more than I possibly *could* know. I must learn to be comfortable *not knowing* any number of things that potentially would be interesting or even crucial to know—such as what was in the box in Owen's study labeled "Please destroy without opening." Every time I am tempted to speculate about what was in that box, I remind myself that *I do not know*, and that when I found it I decided to be content *not knowing*.

August 9, 2015

Today in church I cried when Owen's memorial was announced, thinking desperately, "I can't do this, I can't do this." I need to find the strength to do calmly what needs to be done. I thought I couldn't pick up Owen's ashes from the mortuary, that I couldn't bear to receive my husband in a box. I felt panic in anticipation, but when the time came, I just did it "without ostentation and without weakness," as Jean Jacques Rousseau said. It had to be done.

August 18, 2015

My dementia diaries evolved from keeping track of Owen's uncharacteristic behavior into keeping track of myself against being overwhelmed and collapsing into others' interpretations of dementia. I am deeply fatigued because Owen's death was preceded by the long goodbye—years of physical and emotional exhaustion. Like Beowulf, I needed to remind myself to look for the "fine sword" on the wall with which to confront the monster, dementia.

September 23, 2015

I realized today that when I began to love Owen with the same love with which I had loved my little children, I loved him with a new intensity. I had struggled for several years to continue to love him as my adult companion, but that made his decline constantly frustrating and disappointing to me. As my sister said, he simply no longer was my companion. When I finally gave up and began to love him as my beloved child, I no longer had unrealistic expectations and could love him as he was. The little child that Owen was in his last months was affectionate and loving, easily delighted. That is the Owen I mourn. Not the Owen I married thirty-four years ago, and not the Owen of a decade ago in early stages of dementia, with baffling and hurtful behavior. It is the old Owen, so sweet, so loving, so appreciative of anything and everything I did for him that I miss, mourn, and of whom I have happy memories.

> Love is stronger than death. Since, by the power of his love, God's strength has been made weak to death, love is no longer strong as death, but stronger than death.
>
> —Guerric of Igny

In conclusion, I repeat Owen's neurologist: "Now that we can do something to prevent or cure strokes, heart attacks, and even cancer, we are *all* going to live out into the dementia years. The public should know more about it." Because dementia is increasingly a *social* as well as a personal concern, education about the disease, its symptoms, and the behavior it is likely to prompt is key to reducing the fear, feelings of helplessness, and loneliness experienced by dementia victims and those who love them. Books can give a balanced picture of dementia. Popular films (such as the 2015 movie *Still Alice*) can demonstrate loving ways to families who care for and accompany dementia patients. Bystanders who are puzzled or offended by dementia patients can learn not to take well documented dementia behavior personally.

Because most people avoid information and discussion of dementia until they are personally impacted by a friend or family member's dementia, support groups cannot educate enough people to influence public culture. Rather, concentrated efforts to educate American society about the disease and its effects must occur not only in small support groups for caregivers and family members, but also in the social media communication of our society. American media have had an enormous effect in altering public attitudes toward cigarette smoking. The same kind of mainstreamed education "campaign" could have similar effects in preparing our society to understand and treat lovingly the millions of Americans who will "live out into the dementia years" in the twenty-first century.

March 2, 2016
Berkeley, California

BIBLIOGRAPHY

Arendt, Hannah. *The Life of the Mind.* Vol. 1, *Thinking.* New York: Harcourt, Brace, and Jovanovich, 1978.

Augustine. *Confessions.* Translated by Rex Warner. New York: Mentor Omega, 1963.

———. *Ten Homilies on the First Epistle of St. John.* In *Augustine's Later Works,* edited by John Burnaby. Philadelphia: Westminster, 1955.

Beowulf. Translated by David Wright. Baltimore: Penguin, 1957.

Braver, Barbara, ed. *I Have Called You Friends: Reflections on* Reconciliation. Cambridge, MA: Cowley, 2006.

Camus, Alfred. *The Stranger.* New York: Vintage, 1942.

Carruthers, Mary. *The Craft of Thought: Meditation, Rhetoric, and the Making of Images, 400–1200.* New York: Cambridge University Press, 1998.

Cole, Diane. "A Parent's Worst Fear." Review of *Stronger than Death,* by Sue Chance. *New York Times,* March 29, 1992, 11.

Didion, Joan. *The Year of Magical Thinking.* New York: Knopf, 2005.

Eliot, T. S. "Ash Wednesday." In *Collected Poems, 1909–1935,* 109–21. New York: Harcourt, Brace, 1963.

Epic of Gilgamesh. Translated by N. K. Sandars. Baltimore: Penguin, 1960.

Erdrich, Louise. *The Painted Drum.* New York: HarperCollins, 2005.

Foucault, Michel. *The Foucault Reader.* Edited by Paul Rabinow. New York: Pantheon, 1984.

Gaines, James R. "Liftoff in Coalwood." Review of *Rocket Boys: A Memoir,* by Homer H. Hickam Jr. *New York Times Book Review,* October 19, 1998, 38.

Gawande, Atul. *Being Mortal: Medicine and What Matters in the End.* New York: Henry Holt, 2014.

Hadot, Pierre. *Philosophy as a Way of Life: Spiritual Exercises from Socrates to Foucault.* Edited by Arnold Davidson. Translated by Michael Chase. Oxford: Blackwell, 1995.

Hellenga, Robert. *The Confessions of Frances Godwin.* New York: Bloomsbury, 2014.

Henry, Paul. "Introduction." In *The Enneads,* translated by Stephen MacKenna. 4th ed., revised by B. S. Page. London: Faber, 1969.

Hill, Kathleen. *Who Occupies This House?* Evanston: Northwestern University Press, 2010.

Hustvedt, Siri. *The Sorrows of an American: A Novel.* New York: Henry Holt, 2008.

Johnston, Wayne. *The Navigator of New York.* New York: Doubleday, 2002.

Jung, Carl. *Modern Man in Search of a Soul.* New York: Harcourt & Brace, 1939.

Lamott, Anne. *Bird by Bird: Some Instructions on Writing and Life.* New York: Anchor, 1995.

Malcolm, Janet. "The Silent Woman—I, II, III." *New Yorker*, August 23, 1993.

McFarland, Dennis. *The Singing Boy.* New York: Henry Holt, 2000.

McGrath, Patrick. *Trauma.* New York: Knopf, 2008.

Mercier, Pascal. *Night Train to Lisbon.* Translated by Barbara Harshav. New York: Grove, 2004.

Merwin, W. S. "Words From a Totem Animal." In *Migration: New and Selected Poems.* Port Townsend, WA: Copper Canyon, 2005.

Miles, Margaret R. *Augustine and the Fundamentalist's Daughter.* Eugene, OR: Cascade, 2011.

Miringoff, Marc, and Marque-Luisa Miringoff. *The Social Health of the Nation, 1999.*

Morrison, Toni. *Jazz.* New York: Knopf, 1992.

Murdoch, Iris. *Metaphysics as a Guide to Morals.* London: Chatto and Windus, 1992.

Nussbaum, Martha. *The Therapy of Desire: Theory and Practice in Hellenistic Ethics.* Princeton: Princeton University Press, 1994.

Opdycke, Sandra, and Marque-Luisa Miringoff, *The Social Health of the States, 2008.*

Plotinus. *Enneads.* Translated by A. H. Armstrong. Cambridge, MA: Harvard University Press, 1967.

Rilke, Rainer Maria. *Duino Elegies.* New York: Norton, 1939.

———. *Sonnets to Orpheus.* Translated by C. F. MacIntyre. Berkeley: University of California Press, 1964.

Sarton, May. "Surfers." In *A Durable Fire: New Poems.* New York: Norton, 1972.

Schuld, Joyce. *Foucault, Augustine, and the Hermeneutics of Fragility.* Notre Dame: University of Notre Dame Press, 2002.

Setterfield, Diane. *The Thirteenth Tale.* New York: Washington Square Press, 2006.

Smith, Lee. *News of the Spirit.* New York: Putnam, 1983.

Strauss, Gerald. *Luther's House of Learning: Indoctrination of the Young in the German Reformation.* Baltimore: Johns Hopkins University Press, 1978.

Thomas, Dylan. *Under Milk Wood: A Play for Voices.* New York: New Directions, 1954.

Wieseltier, Leon. "Saul Bellow's Quest for the Sublime Vernacular." *New York Times Sunday Book Review*, November 11, 2010. http://www.nytimes.com/2010/11/21/books/review/Wieseltier-t.html?_r=0.

CPSIA information can be obtained
at www.ICGtesting.com
Printed in the USA
LVHW092208290519
619527LV00001B/245/P

9 781498 282383